Skill Up: A Software Developer's Guide to Life and Career

65 steps to becoming a better developer

Jordan Hudgens

Packt>

BIRMINGHAM - MUMBAI

Skill Up: A Software Developer's Guide to Life and Career

First published: July 2017

Production reference: 1280717

Published by Packt Publishing Ltd.
Livery Place
35 Livery Street
Birmingham B3 2PB, UK.
ISBN 978-1-78728-703-7

www.packtpub.com

Credits

Author

Jordan Hudgens

Acquisition Editor

Ben Renow-Clarke

Content Development Editor

Radhika Atitkar

Technical Editor

Joel D'souza

Proofreader

Safis Editing

Indexer

Pratik Shirodkar

Production Coordinator

Arvindkumar Gupta

Cover Work

Arvindkumar Gupta

About the Author

Jordan Hudgens is the CTO and founder of DevCamp, where he leads instruction and curriculum development for all the DevCamp and Bottega code schools around the US.

As a developer over the past decade, Jordan has traveled the world building applications and training individuals on a wide variety of topics, including Ruby development, big data analysis, and software engineering.

Jordan focuses on project-driven education as opposed to theory-based development. This style of teaching is conducive to learning how to build real-world products that adhere to industry best practices.

Additionally, Jordan has published multiple books on programming and computer science along with developing training curriculum for Learn.co, DevCamp, and AppDev on the topics, namely Ruby on Rails, Java, AngularJS, NoSQL, API development, and algorithms.

www.PacktPub.com

eBooks, discount offers, and more

Did you know that Packt offers eBook versions of every book published, with PDF and ePub files available? You can upgrade to the eBook version at www.PacktPub.com and as a print book customer, you are entitled to a discount on the eBook copy. Get in touch with us at customercare@packtpub.com for more details.

At www.PacktPub.com, you can also read a collection of free technical articles, sign up for a range of free newsletters and receive exclusive discounts and offers on Packt books and eBooks.

Mapt

https://www.packtpub.com/mapt

Get the most in-demand software skills with Mapt. Mapt gives you full access to all Packt books and video courses, as well as industry-leading tools to help you plan your personal development and advance your career.

Why subscribe?

- Fully searchable across every book published by Packt
- Copy and paste, print, and bookmark content
- On demand and accessible via a web browser

Customer Feedback

Thanks for purchasing this Packt book. At Packt, quality is at the heart of our editorial process. To help us improve, please leave us an honest review on this book's Amazon page at https://www.amazon.com/dp/1787287033.

If you'd like to join our team of regular reviewers, you can e-mail us at customerreviews@packtpub.com. We award our regular reviewers with free eBooks and videos in exchange for their valuable feedback. Help us be relentless in improving our products!

To my sweet and loving daughter, Kristine. I cherished every moment of writing this book at coffee shops all over the country with you!

Table of Contents

Preface	**xv**
Part 1: Coder Skills	**1**
Chapter 1: Discovering the Tipping Point for Developers	**3**
Tipping point for developers	3
My own experience	4
The doubt machine	4
The painful process	4
The tipping point(s)	4
The first tipping point	5
The second tipping point	5
The secret	5
The book	6
The solution	6
Chapter 2: Are Developers Born or Made? – Debunking the Myth of Prodigies	**7**
Are prodigies real?	7
The Mozart case study	7
Are developers born or made?	8
The tipping point	8
Why we love the prodigy myth	8
Chapter 3: Do You Have to Be a Genius to Be a Developer?	**11**
The running man	12
Do you have to be a genius to be a developer?	12

The way the mind works   12
The reason   13
A smarter approach   13

Chapter 4: How to Study and Understand Complex Topics?   15

A system for how to study   15

Chapter 5: Effective Study Practices for Developers   17

Why traditional study habits don't work   17
An effective study practices case study   18
The reification example   18
The hard way   19
Additional negative effects   19
The comprehensive study system   19
Summary   20

Chapter 6: Defining Deep Work and What It Means for Developers   21

Definition of deep work   22
The deep work strategy for developers   22
Taking action   22
Removing distractions   22
Study hard and smart   23
Multiple sessions   23
Summary   24

Chapter 7: Task Switching Costs for Developers   25

A system for decreasing task switching costs   26

Chapter 8: How to Use Willpower Limits Instead of Letting Them Use You?   27

What are willpower limits?   27
How many decisions do you make each day?   28
Why is willpower important?   28
Are willpower limits real?   29
When the willpower well runs dry   29
Saving up willpower   29
One outfit to rule them all   30
Being a copycat   30
Focusing willpower   30
Summary   31

Chapter 9: Cramming Versus Consistent Study and a Study System that Works   33

Chapter 10: Is Reading Important for Developers?   37

Why is reading important for developers?   37

CEOs and reading   37

Compounded learning   37

A compounded learning case study   38

The CEO who didn't have time to read   38

My reading system   39

The reading schedule   39

Audio books are books too!   39

Books are too expensive   39

Summary   40

Chapter 11: Learning How to Code – Getting Past Skill Plateaus   41

What is a learning plateau?   41

False ceiling   42

Getting past skill plateaus   42

Proper information/resources   42

Best practices   42

Challenging/new tasks   43

Frustration = skill   43

Summary   44

Chapter 12: Developer Learning Curve – Why Learning How to Code Takes So Long   45

Chapter 13: Slowing Down to Learn How to Code Faster   53

Learn how to code faster   53

Our default mind   54

Hacking the mind   54

Slowing it down   54

Bend it like Beethoven   55

From classical music to coding   55

A practical system   55

Chapter 14: Mental Models for Learning How to Code and Improve as a Developer   57

Mental models for the Kouros   58

What are mental models?	58
Mental models for developers	59
Summary	**59**

Chapter 15: A Developer's Guide for Hacking Procrastination to Achieve Success | 61

Root causes of procrastination	**61**
Hacking procrastination	**62**
Hacking perfectionism	62
Hacking the fear of success	63
Hacking the plan	63
Summary	**64**

Chapter 16: The Problem with Procrastination for Developers | 65

The problem with procrastination	**65**
Instant gratification	66
Baby steps to knock out procrastination	66
Baby coding steps	67

Chapter 17: Practical Ways to Use the Pomodoro Technique as a Developer | 69

Practical ways to use the Pomodoro Technique	**69**
Taking a break	70
Lifestyle versus fads	70
A lifestyle of productivity	71
Practical implementation	**71**

Chapter 18: The Power of Making Mistakes – Learning by Failing | 73

The secret weapon to mastery – making mistakes	**73**
Making mistakes – memory steroids	74
Mistakes force learning	74
Mistakes kill pride	74
Summary	**75**

Chapter 19: Learn How to Code – The Guide to Memorization | 77

The guide to memorization	**77**
Repetition	78
Smarter, not harder	78
Visual mental mapping	78

Short-term versus long-term memory 79
Implementing visual mental mapping 80
Taking a real-world example 81
Finding patterns 81
Copy and paste is the enemy 82
Not everything has to be memorized **83**

Chapter 20: A System for Learning a New Programming Language **85**

Chapter 21: Development Study Tips – Reverse Note-Taking **87**
The problem with traditional note-taking **87**
Reverse note-taking 88
Benefits of reverse note-taking 88
Narrowed focus 88
Story-based mindset 89
Forced repetition 89
Summary **90**

Part 2: Freelancer Skills **91**

Chapter 22: Tips for Organically Growing a Freelance Business **93**
Organically growing a freelance business **93**
Referral requests 94
Blogging 94
Expert positioning 95
Open source contribution 95
Social media marketing 96
Summary **96**

Chapter 23: Freelancing Tips – Knowing When to Fire a Client **97**
My urgent client **97**
When to fire a client 98
#1 – being treated like an employee 98
#2 – tyranny of urgent 98
#3 – toxic environment 99
The joy of firing a client **99**

Chapter 24: Dodging Silver Bullets for
Scalable Freelance Projects   **101**
  The problem with silver bullets   **101**
    Silver bullet customization   102
    Becoming a sharp shooter with code libraries   103

Chapter 25: A Freelance Guide to Managing
Advanced Features   **105**
  Managing advanced features   **105**
  The talent pool   **106**
  The process   **106**
    Kanban   107
  The result   **107**
  Summary   **107**
  A caveat   **108**

Chapter 26: Freelancer Interviews – Practical
Tips for Taking Over a Legacy Application   **109**

Chapter 27: Five Tips for Taking Over a Legacy
Application   **111**
  Tips for taking over a legacy application   **112**
    Creating a test suite   112
    Adding new features via TDD   112
    Breaking out specific features into microservices   112
    DRY up the codebase   113
  Summary   **113**

Chapter 28: Guide to Freelancing – Starting
Over Versus Refactoring   **115**
  The legacy scenario   **115**
  Starting over versus refactoring   **116**
    #1 – removing the fear factor   116
    #2 – analyzing the 80/20 principle   116
    #3 – building an automated bug list   117
    #4 – becoming the client   117
  When should you start over?   **118**
  Summary   **118**

Chapter 29: Should You Use TDD on Freelance Projects? – Comparing Quality Versus Speed   **119**

  Quality versus Speed   **120**

  TDD on freelance projects   **121**

    Making the decision   121

      Giving no choice   121

      Letting the client decide   121

      Using common sense   122

Chapter 30: Automating Client Updates as a Freelance Developer   **123**

  Importance of daily updates   **123**

    An example of client update   124

    Automating client updates   124

    Version control to the rescue   124

  Summary   **125**

Chapter 31: Freelance Requirement Elicitation – A Guide for Feature Development   **127**

  Freelance requirement elicitation   **128**

    How it started   128

    The build   128

    The problem   129

    Who was at fault?   129

  A better way   **129**

    Step 1   129

    Step 2   130

  A better ending   **130**

  Summary   **130**

Chapter 32: How to Remotely Demo Work for Freelance Clients?   **131**

  Why proper demonstrations are important   **131**

  Review of services to remotely demo work   **132**

    Screencast   132

    A remote desktop   133

    PowerPoint   134

  Summary   **135**

Chapter 33: Defining Project Success as a Freelance Developer — 137

A clear end — 137
What is scope creep? — 137
When scope creep isn't scope creep — 138
When scope creep goes badly — 138
Based on requirements — 138
Based on a story — 139
The sign off — 139
Summary — 139

Chapter 34: Top Project Management Tools for Freelancers — 141

Top project management tools — 141
Basecamp — 142
Trello — 144
LeanKit — 145
ProWorkflow — 146
Wrike — 146
GitHub — 147
Summary — 148

Chapter 35: Top Freelance Bookkeeping Options for Developers — 149

Freelance bookkeeping options — 149
FreshBooks — 150
How it works — 151
FreshBooks additional features — 152
Weaknesses — 152
QuickBooks — 152
NetSuite — 153
Summary — 153

Chapter 36: Learning the Secret to Get New Clients as a Freelancer — 155

Where to find new clients — 155
The challenge in getting new clients with outsourcing services — 156
Getting new clients as a freelancer — 157
Proposal material — 157
Sending out constant proposals — 157

The result   158
Summary   **158**
**Chapter 37: Managing Client Conflicts
as a Freelancer**   **159**
Strategies for managing client conflicts   159
**Chapter 38: Examples of Freelance Portfolios
That Help Acquire New Clients**   **163**
Examples of freelance portfolios   163
Social network utility   164
An API tool   164
An accounting application   164
A scheduling application   164
A frontend application   164
**Chapter 39: Importance of Test-Driven
Development for Coders**   **167**
Importance of test-driven development   169
Summary   **171**
**Chapter 40: SEO Best Practices and Strategies
for Freelancers**   **173**
SEO best practices tutorial   173
Content is king   173
Creating an XML sitemap   174
Mixing text, images, and videos   174
Managing your site speed   174
Site responsiveness   174
Backlinks   175
Focused content   175
Summary   **175**
Chapter 41: Client Communication Freelancing Tips **177**
A system to maintain proper client communication   178
Summary   **178**
**Chapter 42: Outsource Web Developers Properly
with System-Based Processes**   **179**
A system to manage outsourced web developers   180
Summary   **180**

Chapter 43: How to Create Accurate Freelance Bids?   **181**
Summary   182

**Chapter 44: Freelancer Tips – Three Ways to
Get New Clients**   **183**
Freelancing services   183
LinkedIn   184
Referrals   184
Summary   184

Part 3: Career Skills   **185**

**Chapter 45: Should I Learn to Code? – A Balanced
Perspective on Programming**   **187**
Should I learn to code? – a balanced look at both sides   188
Summary   189

**Chapter 46: Following Your Passion – Good or
Bad Advice for Developers?**   **191**
Following your passion – a case study   191
Summary   192

**Chapter 47: How to Learn to Code from
Scratch? – A Practical Strategy**   **193**
Small bites   193
Tutorials   194
Reading   195
Real-world projects   196
Coding is hard   196
But you can learn programming   196

Chapter 48: How to Choose a Developer Specialty?   **197**
How to choose a developer specialty?   197
#1 – the full stack developer   198
#2 – the server-side developer   198
#3 – the frontend developer   199
#4 – the mobile developer   199
#5 – the data scientist   200
Making the decision   **200**

Chapter 49: How to Choose Your Next
Programming Language?   **203**
How to pick a programming language?   **203**
The next job you want   204
Your specialty   204
Specialty-based mapping   205
Summary   **206**

Chapter 50: Developer Soft Skills – Learning
How to Gain an Edge in the Marketplace   **207**
Developer soft skills   **207**
Writing   208
Conversation   208
Conversation tips   208
Management   209
Design   209
Public speaking   210
Becoming a better public speaker   211
The importance of soft skills   **211**

Chapter 51: Developer Learning
Options – A Practical Analysis   **213**
Degrees of programming expertise   **213**
Becoming a professional developer   **213**
Developer bootcamps   214
Is this practical?   214
Improving your skill in your current profession **215**
Is this practical?   215
Learning for fun or as a hobby   **216**
Summary   **216**

Chapter 52: Is it Possible to Lose
Your Coding Skills?   **217**
Summary   **219**

Chapter 53: Is Writing Bad Code Immoral
for Developers?   **221**
How to write better code   223
Summary   223

Chapter 54: Inspirational Programming Advice from Howard Roark   225

Chapter 55: Best Practices Versus Creativity as a Developer   227

Chapter 56: A Practical Guide to Approaching Project Development   231

Student question   231
Strategies to approaching project development   232
  Planning a feature from start to end   232
  Moving from requirements to stories   232
  Starting with a base case   233
  Fear of the unknown   233
    Moving fast and breaking things   234
  Battling procrastination   234
  Small, practical steps   234
  Getting unstuck   235
    Application bugs   235
    Messages over models   235

Chapter 57: How to Practice Programming Techniques and Improve as a Developer?   237

Engaging in pair programming   237
Utilizing open source software   238
Visiting the DailyProgrammer subreddit on Reddit   238
Taking online courses   238
Code katas   239
Summary   239

Chapter 58: What Does It Take to Become a Great Developer?   241

Tips for becoming a great developer   241
  Working through difficult features   242
  Community contribution   242
  Artistry   243
  Craftsmanship   243
    Steve Jobs's craftsmanship   244
  Adapting to change   244
  Tireless learning   245
Summary   246

Chapter 59: How to Stay Sharp as a Developer?   247

Tips to stay sharp as a developer   247

#1 – coding exercises   247

Example coding exercises   248

#2 – teaching others to code   249

How does this apply to development?   249

#3 – reading   250

#4 – newsletters   250

#5 – tutorials   250

Summary   250

Chapter 60: Developer Resume Tips – How to Create an Effective Resume?   251

Developer resume tips   251

Keep it simple   251

Keep it relatable   252

Keep it professional   253

Summary   253

Chapter 61: Developer Salary Negotiation Strategies   255

Knowing your skill set   255

Knowing the industry   255

Knowing the organization   256

Researching salary rates   256

Chapter 62: Best Questions to Ask During a Job Interview   257

Best questions to ask during a job interview   258

Poor questions to ask during a job interview   259

Summary   260

Chapter 63: Answering in an Impossible Interview   261

Questions   261

Answering impossible interview questions – case studies   261

Chapter 64: Greatest Weakness Answers for Coding Interviews   263

Bad answers to your greatest weakness   263

Good answers to your greatest weakness   264

Chapter 65: Enterprise Software Job Strategy and Guide 265

Summary 266

Index 267

Preface

Skill Up: A Software Developer's Guide to Life and Career is an all-purpose toolkit for your programming career. It has been built by Jordan Hudgens over a lifetime of coding and teaching coding. It helps you identify the key questions and stumbling blocks that programmers encounter, and gives you the answers to them! It is a comprehensive guide containing more than 50 insights and methodologies that you can use to improve the work you produce, and to give advice in your day-to-day career.

Focusing on your life skills and the key soft skills we need in the modern world, *Skill Up: A Software Developer's Guide to Life and Career* will help you find your path to being a better and a happier coder.

What this book covers

Part 1, Coder Skills, contains advice for people starting out in a coding career, or those who are already working as in a programming role but want to improve their general skills. It includes such subjects as how to study and understand complex topics, defining deep work and what it means for developers, and getting past skill plateaus when learning new languages.

Part 2, Freelancer Skills, contains advice for developers working as freelancers and trying to manage their careers and bid on new tenders. It includes such subjects as knowing when to fire a client, practical tips for taking over legacy applications, and a guide to automating client update messages.

Part 3, Career Skills, contains advice for having a successful career as a developer. It provides information on how to advance your career, and practical tips, such as interview guides. It includes such subjects as how to practice programming techniques and improve as a developer, how to balance best practice and creativity as a developer, and developer salary negotiation strategies.

Who this book is for

This book is useful for programmers of any ability or discipline. It has advice for those thinking about beginning a career in programming, those already working as a fully employed programmer, and for those working as freelance developers.

Conventions

In this book, you will find a number of text styles that distinguish between different kinds of information. Here are some examples of these styles and an explanation of their meaning.

Code words in text, database table names, folder names, filenames, file extensions, pathnames, dummy URLs, user input, and Twitter handles are shown as follows: "Returning to our case study of memorizing CSS elements, let's look at the border attributes available in CSS3: `border`."

New terms and **important words** are shown in bold. Words that you see on the screen, for example, in menus or dialog boxes, appear in the text like this: "Here in the image I would move a task from being a **To-Do**, to being **Assigned**, to **Working**, to **Under Review**, and finally to **Finished**."

Reader feedback

Feedback from our readers is always welcome. Let us know what you think about this book—what you liked or disliked. Reader feedback is important for us as it helps us develop titles that you will really get the most out of.

To send us general feedback, simply e-mail `feedback@packtpub.com`, and mention the book's title in the subject of your message.

If there is a topic that you have expertise in and you are interested in either writing or contributing to a book, see our author guide at `www.packtpub.com/authors`.

Customer support

Now that you are the proud owner of a Packt book, we have a number of things to help you to get the most from your purchase.

Errata

Although we have taken every care to ensure the accuracy of our content, mistakes do happen. If you find a mistake in one of our books—maybe a mistake in the text or the code—we would be grateful if you could report this to us. By doing so, you can save other readers from frustration and help us improve subsequent versions of this book. If you find any errata, please report them by visiting http://www.packtpub.com/submit-errata, selecting your book, clicking on the **Errata Submission Form** link, and entering the details of your errata. Once your errata are verified, your submission will be accepted and the errata will be uploaded to our website or added to any list of existing errata under the Errata section of that title.

To view the previously submitted errata, go to https://www.packtpub.com/books/content/support and enter the name of the book in the search field. The required information will appear under the **Errata** section.

Piracy

Piracy of copyrighted material on the Internet is an ongoing problem across all media. At Packt, we take the protection of our copyright and licenses very seriously. If you come across any illegal copies of our works in any form on the Internet, please provide us with the location address or website name immediately so that we can pursue a remedy.

Please contact us at copyright@packtpub.com with a link to the suspected pirated material.

We appreciate your help in protecting our authors and our ability to bring you valuable content.

Questions

If you have a problem with any aspect of this book, you can contact us at questions@packtpub.com, and we will do our best to address the problem.

Part 1

Coder Skills

1
Discovering the Tipping Point for Developers

If you've been programming for a while, a question that has most likely crossed your mind is this:

"Am I a good developer?"

Before we go on, let me share a little secret with you... Every developer, even senior developers, have insecurities when it comes to programming. Few individuals like to share that information, mainly because confidence and even arrogance has become a developer stereotype for some stupid reason.

However, I won't BS you. I can tell you that the more experience I have as a coder, the more I realize how much more there is to learn and how far I still have to go.

Tipping point for developers

With all that being said, I want to discuss topic of defining the tipping point for developers, which is essentially the point at which a developer goes from a beginner to a pro. Since this topic is a bit abstract, it's not possible to point to a specific point in time and say:

"Here it is, this is when it all clicks and makes sense."

There's not a sentinel moment when programming mastery occurs. It's different for every individual.

My own experience

I remember when I was originally learning programming. Understanding the syntax and context did not come easy for me. It seemed like I spent 99% of my time looking things up and copying and pasting code from others just to get my programs running.

The doubt machine

Needless to say, my confidence as a programmer was very low in the beginning. I kept being plagued by nagging doubts, such as:

- Maybe programming isn't for you
- Even if you code works you won't be able to write your own programs
- You're only typing in what the book is saying to do, you won't be able to build anything custom

And the negative thoughts continued from there

The painful process

If you're a new developer maybe some of this sounds familiar to you, or maybe it doesn't and I simply lacked confidence. Either way, I trudged along, trying everything I could think of to improve as a developer:

- Going through dozens upon dozens of programming books in various languages
- Trying to build up a portfolio of project
- Following online guides

However, back when I was originally learning how to code, the online resources weren't quite as good as they are today.

The tipping point(s)

So, what did the trick and pushed me over the edge to become a professional developer? None of those things… and all those things. I persevered through project after project and I consumed every training resource I could find. And slowly something amazing started to happen:

"Everything started to make sense."

Chapter 1

The first tipping point

Even though it was a while ago, I still remember the moment my first development tipping point happened. I was sitting in front of my computer in a coffee shop and working on a web application.

A few hours went by and I stopped dead in my tracks, realizing that I had just spent the afternoon building a project and hadn't looked up a single code snippet. It wasn't like I programmed the space station, the project was incredibly basic. However, it was one of the most exciting moments I can remember in my life.

The second tipping point

As great as that was, I still had very far to go. I remember the next moment when I felt like I reached another key milestone. Even though my confidence had increased as a developer, the thought of anyone seeing my code was a very scary thought. However, I had started to build my freelance business and a client (who was also a developer) asked me to perform a pair programming session with him.

He had run into a bug with the program we were building and asked me to jump on a screen sharing session where we could work on the project at the same time. Honestly, I was scared to death when he asked. I had never coded in front of anyone before and the thought of doing it with this client pretty much gave me a panic attack. However, I didn't really have a choice in the matter so I started the session with him. After a few minutes of nervousness, I started to relax and to my surprise not only did I not make a fool of myself, I actually figured out the bug in his code and got the feature working.

The secret

So, what was my secret to getting over the hump and going from a beginner to a professional developer? Unfortunately, there is no easy-to-follow recipe. However, there is a process that is guaranteed to work. And the process isn't specific to becoming a programmer, it's the same whether you want to be a developer or a professional athlete... it's hard and smart work.

The book

In the book *The Tipping Point*, by *Malcolm Gladwell*, Gladwell gives countless case studies of what it takes for individuals to achieve mastery in a specific field. The key comes down to how dedicated an individual is to a specific skill. The book postulates that it takes around 10,000 hours for an individual to become a true master of whatever they're pursuing.

I'm not sure I believe in the 10,000-hour rule, mainly because there are a large number of variables when it comes to learning a topic or skill and rarely does a single rule apply for all fields. Also, I think the quality of your practice makes a significant difference.

For example, if you're learning how to play the violin: 5,000 hours of practice with a world class instructor is probably equivalent to 10,000 hours trying to figure it out yourself. However, with all that being said, one thing cannot be denied, *the key to mastery is hard work*.

The solution

I'm sorry if you were hoping for a quick fix. I can tell you from experience that there are no shortcuts to becoming a developer. You need to learn:

- The fundamentals of coding
- How to build projects on your own
- Various process for working through bugs

Becoming a great developer is not an easy road. However, be comforted in the fact that you are 100% in control of how skilled you will become. The formula is straightforward: the harder you work, the better you will get. So, get your hands on all the material you can find on the language and framework you want to learn. Work through challenging applications and you will be well on your way to mastery.

And soon you will be able to have the exciting moment of clarity when everything starts to click.

2
Are Developers Born or Made? – Debunking the Myth of Prodigies

When talking to development students, I've discovered one topic that constantly arises in conversation. And that topic is the misconceived notion that great developers are born with a special programming gene. So, let's walk through the question *are developers born or made*, from a practical perspective.

Are prodigies real?

Before tackling this question, let's take a step back and discuss the topic of prodigies. Because whenever someone thinks that a certain group of individuals are born with superhuman-like talent, they're essentially saying that these special people are prodigies.

The Mozart case study

But are prodigies real? Let's take a look at one of the most famous prodigies of all time, Mozart. At the age of 5, Mozart was playing concert grade music to the royal family. Surely, this would qualify Mozart as a prodigy, right?

In his book, *Peak: Secrets from the New Science of Expertise*, researcher *Anders Ericsson* dispels a number of commonly held prodigy myths. He had this to say about Mozart:

> *"If you compare the kind of music pieces that Mozart can play at various ages to today's Suzuki-trained children, he is not exceptional. If anything, he's relatively average."*

In his book, Ericsson dedicates a full chapter to debunking the concept of prodigies. And in each case, he illustrates that the individuals achieved their respective levels of success through massage amounts of work.

Are developers born or made?

Extending the Mozart case study, let's discuss how this applies to developers. Whenever we see a skilled coder it's easy to think that they were born with the innate ability to build applications and that learning new languages and frameworks comes easy to them.

However, nothing could be further from the truth. Over the years I've known more developers than I can count and I have yet to find a single one that was a born developer. I know programmers that work for Google and Amazon, along with computer science professors who specialize in research that boggles my mind to think about. And as amazing as all of these individuals are, each one of them became a great developer through hard work and dedication.

The tipping point

In *Chapter 1, Discovering the Tipping Point for Developers* I've discussed the tipping point for developers. The longer I teach and the more I work on my own coding skills, the more I'm convinced that the key to excellence is as straightforward as focused practice.

If you want to become a skilled developer badly enough, and you're willing to:

- Dedicate the time
- Learn from experienced teachers
- Fight through frustrating challenges
- Continually build projects with features you've never developed before

You're going to wake up one day and realize that everything is clicking and that you've become a professional programmer.

Why we love the prodigy myth

Before I end this chapter, I want to address a subtle issue that explains the reason of why we, as humans, love the idea of prodigies.

Chapter 2

The concept of prodigies, individuals born with a natural ability to be successful at a certain skill, such as sports, math, or programming, can be detrimental to our own success. This belief is dangerous because it causes our minds to have negative responses to failure.

For example, if you're an aspiring developer who thinks that programmers are born and not made, when you come across a bug that you can't seem to figure out or a feature you can't build, your first reaction might be:

I guess I wasn't born to do be a developer.

Or:

I wish I had talent like XYZ programmer, everything seems to come so easy to him.

If you catch yourself with thoughts like these, remind yourself that prodigies aren't real.

Developers achieve greatness through smart work and perseverance. The 10,000-hour rule from the *Tipping Point* book by *Malcolm Gladwell* may not be exactly accurate. However, it does give a general guide for how much work is required to reach a level of mastery.

If you feel like you weren't born with the "developer gene", go and knock out 10,000 hours of focused practice on building applications. I think you'll be pleasantly surprised to find that you'll become so good, that other people will look at you, and they'll think… that you were just born this way.

3

Do You Have to Be a Genius to Be a Developer?

We've discussed the topic of whether great developers are born or made. And in this chapter, we're going to look at a similar topic from a different angle. And we're going to answer the question *do you have to be a genius to be a developer?*

Because of the near-magical nature of coding, one of the most common remarks I hear from individuals who hear what I do is:

"Oh wow, you're so smart!"

In fact, just recently I traveled to meet with a group of developers and the head of the company introduced me by saying:

"This is Jordan, he's just here to be smart."

I know that when people say things like this it comes from a good place. However, it bothers me. And it bothers me for a couple reasons:

1. First and foremost, these type of comments make it seem like all it takes to become a great developer is being smart.

2. Following up on the above point, these remarks devalue the countless hours of work that are required to learn development.

The running man

I'm going to get off my soap box for a moment and discuss the life of Steve Prefontaine. If you've never heard of him before, Prefontaine was one of the world's greatest runners during his time. Before tragically dying in a car accident at 24 years old, he had already broken seven track world records.

During his climactic rise to success, many people would try to compliment Prefontaine by saying how talented he was, and by calling him a prodigy, such as on the cover of Sports Illustrated.

However, he was famous for getting furious at people for this type of statement. He said that his success had literally nothing to do with talent. In fact, he said he wasn't born with any innate ability as a runner. Instead he credits 100% of his success with his legendary work ethic.

Do you have to be a genius to be a developer?

It's important to take the same approach that Prefontaine took as developers. If you fall into the trap of thinking that only geniuses can become good coders, it will most likely lead to quitting when tasks become challenging. This is because our minds constantly are searching for ways to work less. And if you believe that being a genius is a requirement for development, you will have a built-in excuse for faltering on your developer learning journey.

The way the mind works

In a comprehensive educational study published in Scientific American (http://www.scientificamerican.com/article/the-secret-to-raising-smart-kids1/), kids were broken into two groups and taken through some academic assignments. Both groups scored around the same for the assignments. One of the groups were praised by their parents and teachers, and the focus of the compliments centered around how smart and talented the kids were.

The second group of students were complimented in a different manner. Instead of complimenting students on their innate ability, students were complimented on how hard they worked.

After going through this cycle of compliments, the same two groups of students were presented with new, and very challenging assignments.

Chapter 3

The first group of students, the ones that had been told that they were brilliant, ended up giving up and not completing the tasks that were assigned to them. However, the second group of students, the ones that were complimented on their hard work, performed dramatically better than group 1.

The reason

So why did two groups of students have such different results when, by all appearances, the students had the same level of actual skill?

The researchers concluded that the students from group 1 felt like the top priority was maintaining their *genius* status. So, they quit the second assignment early because they didn't want to look bad and tarnish the *genius* label that they had been given.

However, the second group of students didn't feel the pressure to maintain a genius status. Instead, they wanted to maintain their new reputations as hard workers. With this mindset, the second set of students worked through the challenging topics instead of giving up.

A smarter approach

So, instead of taking the mindset that you need to be a genius to become a developer, take the mindset that best developers are also the hardest working developers. With this approach, your potential for skill is literally limitless. You are 100% in control of how good you will become as a coder. And your success will completely be determined how hard (and how smart) you are willing to work.

4

How to Study
and Understand
Complex Topics?

When I was younger I used to struggle learning a new or difficult subject, and over the years and about a decade of university and grad school have helped me put together a strategy for how to study and understand complex topics. Typically, I apply this learning system to subjects such as algorithms and software engineering; however, it can be applied to any topic.

While there is a near infinite set of study strategies out there, I like this approach because it utilizes a divide and conquer strategy, focusing on breaking a complex topic into easy-to-understand components, and putting the pieces back together at the end to see how they all work together.

A system for how to study

Let's take a case study example: understanding how logarithms work. Logarithms are used throughout the fields of mathematics and computer science; however, unless you use them regularly it's easy to get rusty on them:

1. The first task that I will do is take a piece of paper and write Logarithm in the center and circle it.

2. Next, I'll go to a comprehensive post on the topic, such as one on Wikipedia. When reading the first sentence, I come across a few terms that are a bit fuzzy:

    ° Inverse operation
    ° Exponentiation

I will stop reading the logarithm article and go and read those two articles until I feel comfortable with what they represent. After I feel good about those two items, I write them as their own circles that connect to the Logarithm circle. I will also add any examples that will help me understand what the terms mean if necessary.

3. Next, I'll go back to the original Logarithm post and keep going through the article repeating this process until the entire page is filled with a mind map that explains each component that makes up logarithms and how they work together. This may include base case examples, such as:

64 = 2^6 is the same as log 2 (64) = 6

If this seems like a dead simple approach to study…it is. The goal of studying is to learn a topic, and one of the easiest ways to understand a complex subject is to break it into easy to comprehend components. For example, if you're trying to understand an advanced algorithm in computer science from scratch, you may feel a little intimidated.

However, if you break the algorithm down into small enough components you'll see that it's essentially a process of steps made up of connecting simple modules such as loops, manipulating variables, and using conditionals. A problem is only hard when you try to think of it as a whole. However, any concept can be understood if you simplify it down to easy to comprehend pieces.

Obviously, the more complex the topic, the longer it will take to deconstruct; however, I am a firm believer that anyone can understand any topic assuming they dedicate themselves and put the work in. I hope that you can leverage this mind mapping process to understand complex topics and that it will help you learn how to study properly and truly learn.

5

Effective Study Practices for Developers

Let's imagine that you're back in school and midterm exams are coming up. How would you study? Some common approaches might be:

- Re-read the study materials or lecture notes
- Highlight and memorize the key terms
- Go over your notes constantly until test day comes

Those all sound like effective study practices. However, cognitive research has shown that many of the traditional study patterns that students have followed for decades simply do not work.

I didn't make up that list of study patterns. That's exactly what I used to do in preparing for exams. However, I discovered (after failing a number of tests) that these strategies failed miserably when it came to helping me to truly learn new concepts.

Why traditional study habits don't work

This type of approach to studying doesn't work because our minds don't function like computers. A computer can take in information and then spit it back out. However, our minds are more relational in nature.

By relational in nature, I mean that our brain functions like a graph-based network. If new information attempts to enter the brain without being connected to any of our previous knowledge, it will simply be rejected.

For example, let's imagine that you are new to learning programming. If you simply run through a list of programming terms and syntax rules, you might memorize them in the short run.

However, because your brain hasn't been properly introduced to the concepts, it will eventually eject the information, viewing it as useless since it's not related to the rest of your view of the world.

However, imagine that you take a different approach. In this new, more enlightened approach, you work with your brain and allow it to connect each of the new programming concepts that you're learning to knowledge and experiences that you already have.

An effective study practices case study

Whenever I'm teaching a new programming concept to students, I try to draw a fitting analogy to a real-world concept. This process is called reification and I view it as one of my most important tasks as a teacher.

Let's imagine that you are learning about the MVC (Model, View, Controller) design pattern in software development. You could take the approach of trying to memorize each of the roles of the Model, View, and Controller. However, that strategy wouldn't help you answer questions related to how each of the components work together. And if you memorize quiz questions and answers, you probably will have issues answering anything that you haven't memorized.

The reification example

What if instead of trying to memorize key terms about the MVC pattern you focused on drawing a real-world analogy to the process? My favorite way to understand this type of architecture is comparing it to a restaurant:

- **Model**: The model is the chef in the kitchen. In the same way that a chef prepares the meal for customers, the model works directly with the data for the application.
- **Controller**: The controller works like a restaurant waiter. In an application, the controller's role is based on taking requests and managing communication between the model and the view. This is much like a waiter who takes customer orders, communicates with the chef, and eventually brings the food out to the table.

Chapter 5

- **View**: The view is like the table that a customer is sitting at. It doesn't do much besides provide a platform for placing the food on. This is exactly like how the view should operate in an application. If built properly, a view should simply be a place where data is shown to users.

Do you see what we just did? We learned about the MVC design pattern in a way that our minds can actually comprehend. I could fall out of bed and recite back the role of each component of the MVC architecture, not because I spent countless hours trying to memorize them, but because I connected the concept to my real-world experiences.

The hard way

Over the years I've concluded that if studying is easy…I'm doing it wrong. I used to follow study pattern of:

1. Read
2. Memorize
3. Repeat

This was partly because it was easy. It wasn't mentally taxing to sit down and read through a textbook or my notes. However, research is proving that this type of study habit is not only ineffective, it is also damaging.

Additional negative effects

How is it damaging? If you have followed this type of study system you know one thing: it takes time. This time spent reading and memorizing could have been used in countless other ways that would have proven more effective in the long run. And when it comes to studying, time is one of the most valuable assets that you have, so wasting it is akin to an educational felony.

The comprehensive study system

In addition to the process of reification, there are a number of other study strategies that research is showing to be more effective than traditional study practices. In their book *Make It Stick*, cognitive psychologists *Brown, Roediger,* and *McDaniel* give the following recommendations for studying:

- When learning from a textbook, use the key terms from the back of each chapter to test yourself.

- List out key terms and use each one in a paragraph; this will test to see if you understand a concept outside of the realm of how the textbook or instructor supplied it.

- While reading new material, convert the main concepts into a series of questions and then go back and answer the questions when you're done reading the chapter.

- Rephrase the main ideas in your own words as you go through the material.

- Relate the main concepts to your own experiences, much like the reification process we've already discussed.

- Look for examples of key concepts outside of the text. When I'm learning a new programming language I never rely on a single source. If I come across a concept that doesn't make sense I'll usually review 2- 3 other sources that provide alternative explanations to what I'm attempting to learn.

Summary

In summary, when it comes to effective study practices, make sure that you're making the most of your time. Remember that the most important goal with studying is retaining knowledge so that you can use it in real-world scenarios. And the best way to accomplish this goal is by following strategies that work with your mind's learning patterns.

6

Defining Deep Work and What It Means for Developers

Standing on the podium, Michael Phelps stares at the American flag and listens to the National Anthem after winning gold once again. After watching Phelps win 21 gold medals (at the time I'm writing this), it's natural to ask: "Was he simply born for greatness?" I don't know. Yes, his body type has helped him take advantage of physical elements of swimming.

However, there are millions of individuals with his height and wingspan who watch him at the Olympics from their couches every four years. There is no magical swimming gene that Phelps was born with. Instead, the secret to his success can be found in his discipline to a practice called *deep work*. Muscle Prodigy (`https://www.muscleprodigy.com/michael-phelps-workout-and-diet/`) research claims:

> *"Phelps swims minimum 80,000 meters a week, which is nearly 50 miles. He practices twice a day, sometimes more if he's training at altitude. Phelps trains for around five to six hours a day at six days a week."*

If Malcom Gladwell's 10,000-hour rule is even close to being accurate, Michael Phelps surpassed this benchmark years ago.

In case you're wondering how this applies to coding, don't worry, I haven't forgotten that this is a show for developers.

Definition of deep work

As you go through these chapters, you may discover that one of my favorite books is *Deep Work* by *Cal Newport*. (The fact I referenced the book a few dozen times may given it away). So, what exactly is deep work? A dead simple explanation of deep work is:

"Deep work is the ability to focus without distraction on a cognitively demanding task."

Whether you believe that swimming is cognitively demanding or not, I believe that Phelps's example is fitting. If you have ever attempted to train with the level of intensity that Phelps does, you can attest to the mental toll that training takes. So essentially, deep work can be simplified by saying that it has the following characteristics:

1. It's a real-world action. It's not a theoretical concept, it's something that you can practically implement.

2. To work properly you have to eliminate 100% of your distractions.

3. The task has to be challenging.

The deep work strategy for developers

Let's dissect the definition of deep work and build a practical strategy for how it can be implemented from a developer perspective. Let's imagine that you want to learn about the computer science topic of asymptotic analysis. If you've never heard of asymptotic analysis, don't worry, you can trust me that it qualifies as a challenging topic.

Taking action

Let's start with the fact that deep work is an action. With that in mind, you will need to make a clearly defined time slot. If you have never practice deep work studying before, I'd recommend limiting the slot to around two hours. As you'll discover deep work is a draining task. For our example, let's imagine that you have designated 9 AM to 11 AM as when you're going to study asymptotic analysis.

Removing distractions

With your time slot set, now it's time to remove any and all potential distractions. Let me be 100% explicit; this means:

1. You cannot check your email.

2. No phone calls. In fact, put your phone in airplane mode to ensure no one calls or text messages you.

Chapter 6

3. Don't even think about checking Instagram, Facebook, Twitter, or Tinder. All your swipe rights will have to wait for a few hours.

If I missed any distractions you can add them to the list. It may also help to listen to classical music to block out any potential sound distractions while you study.

Study hard and smart

Now that you have dedicated a few hours to studying asymptotic analysis and have removed all your distractions, it's finally time to get down to business. If you think that now you can simply start reading a few Wikipedia posts, I'm sorry, that won't earn you a deep work badge.

For deep work to be truly effective, it has to be difficult. If I was learning about asymptotic analysis for the first time and wanted to practice deep work while studying it, I'd take the following approach:

1. I'd begin by reading a number of online resources on the subject.

2. Next I'd watch an online lecture while taking notes.

3. I would then find practice exercises where I would attempt to figure out problems from scratch.

4. Next, I would write a blog post or record myself teaching the concept.

5. Lastly, I would have another student or instructor review my teaching and exercises to ensure that I understood the concept properly.

Do you see how much more comprehensive this type of studying is? Even if you had never heard of asymptotic analysis before your deep work study session, you would be fluent in it after you were done.

Multiple sessions

When I mentioned earlier how you should limit your deep work sessions to around 2 hours, I don't mean that you can understand any topic in that period of time. Some complex topics may take days, weeks, months, or years to properly understand. So, it is completely fine to spend a number of sessions working through the same concept. If you are going to do this, I recommend that you make notes for what you were doing when you stopped. This will allow you to pick up right where you left off.

Summary

I hope that this has been a helpful introduction to what deep work is and how you can practically implement it as a developer. If you want to learn more about the topic I suggest that you pick up Newport's book. It will give you a great set of tools for learning how to use deep work to constantly improve as a developer. When it comes to learning, deep work is the closest thing you can get to steroids. Good luck with the coding!

7
Task Switching Costs for Developers

In this chapter, I'm going to discuss the concept of **task switching costs**. Task switching, commonly referred to as **multitasking**, can be detrimental to your performance as a developer and can even lead to errors in your projects. Our world has changed dramatically over the past decade, whether for good or bad is not a topic we'll discuss in this chapter. However, one thing is sure: we are constantly bombarded with distractions.

As I was researching this chapter, I received over a dozen emails, 7 Snapchat messages, 30 notifications on Instagram, 7 Twitter notifications, 5 Skype instant messages, and surprisingly only 9 text messages. If you were counting, that's around 72 various notifications that were pushed to me in the past two hours. Beyond that, I researched this chapter at a coffee shop filled with potential distractions.

So exactly how bad are distractions? Research from Gloria Mark (https://www.fastcompany.com/944128/worker-interrupted-cost-task-switching), who is a Professor in the Department of Informatics at the UC Irvine, shows that it takes, on average, 23 minutes and 15 seconds to get fully back on task after being distracted. That's a very, very bad thing when it comes to productivity; however, I've seen it myself, I've lost track of how many times I'll be in the middle of a development project and receive an email on a completely unrelated matter and instead of ignoring it and continuing to work I'll read it and then spend time working on another task before returning to the project.

This may not sound like a major issue, except that when I come back to the project, I don't pick up from where I left off. Instead I have to re-familiarize myself with what I was working on the moment that I was distracted. If the problem was complex, it may take me even longer than the 23 minutes in order to get back in the zone and working on the project.

So, in a world filled with emails and social media distractions, how can anyone get any real work done? After reading Cal Newport's book *Deep Work*, I started to put together some practical ways that I can work efficiently and still stay in touch with the world.

A system for decreasing task switching costs

1. If I'm working on a project, I set aside a specific amount of time that morning. For example, if I'm working on Project X for 2 hours, I will put it on my calendar and say that from 9 AM to 11 AM I'm working on Project X.

2. I remove any and all negative distractions during that time. That means I'll usually put my phone on Airplane mode so I don't receive any social media notifications. Notice how I said negative distractions? I made this distinction because in the same research report from UC Irvine it revealed that not all distractions are bad. If the distraction is related to the task that you're working on, it can actually be beneficial. For example, if I'm working on the routing engine for a web application and the client messages me to discuss the application, what they say may actually influence the work that I'm doing or give me an idea on how to refine it. That's a good distraction and it's why I typically will keep my email and instant messenger on while I'm working. However, if I see that the Skype message or email is coming from another client or is completely unrelated I'll simply ignore it. I do know many Deep Work proponents who would say that 100% of your distractions have to be eliminated; however, that's not always practical.

3. Have a clear conclusion for whatever you are studying or working on. If you don't establish an end for the task, your mind is going to be prone to wander in the same way that a runner without a finish line won't be able to effectively compete in a race. The research around task switching costs also reveals that even planned distractions are harmful, so if you are planning on working for 2 hours straight on a project, don't plan any breaks in the middle of the task. Maintain your focus throughout the allotted time and then you'll be free to relax afterwards.

I hope that this has been a helpful overview of task switching costs and that you now have some practical methods for staying on task.

8

How to Use Willpower Limits Instead of Letting Them Use You?

There are a number of common characteristics among great developers. However, few virtues are as important as willpower. World class coders constantly are forced to work through complex concepts, and without willpower they would give up before experiencing any kind of breakthrough. In this chapter, I'm going to walk through the topic of willpower limits.

This will include a practical walk through on:

- What willpower limits are
- How you can improve your personal willpower limits
- A plan for being intentional about managing willpower limits

What are willpower limits?

For graduate school I have performed extensive research on the topic of task switching costs. While studying about task switching, I came across the topic of willpower limits and how they related to performance. Essentially, the study of willpower limits says that *individuals have a limited amount of decision making power each day.*

How many decisions do you make each day?

If that sounds weird to you, don't worry, I had a hard time with the concept right away too. So, let's go through a typical day for a developer. What are some decisions that you make each day?

- Deciding to get up or press snooze on the alarm clock
- Picking out what to eat for breakfast
- Selecting your clothes for the day
- Deciding if you want to go to the gym, a run, or walk around and play Pokémon Go
- Deciding on which route to take to work
- And the list goes on and on

Notice how none of those items are related to development at all. And in fact, those were all common decision items that you have to make each morning before you even get into work. If you actually count the number of decisions that you have to make each day, you'd discover the number is probably in the hundreds or even thousands. If you include subconscious decisions such as staying in your lane while driving, the number is most likely in the millions every day!

Why is willpower important?

Hopefully, I've helped you see all of the decisions that we make daily. So why do willpower limits matter when it comes to making decisions? Mainly because without willpower the quality of our decisions will suffer dramatically.

Imagine yourself without willpower for a second. With no willpower, you:

- Would eat whatever you wanted, harming your overall health
- Wouldn't study, thus never improving as a developer
- Would recklessly spend money on whatever popped into your mind, forcing you into debt and eventually bankruptcy

It's not a pretty picture, which is why willpower is so important when it comes to making decisions. Willpower gives you the self-control to make the right decision, even when it's not the easy one.

Are willpower limits real?

So, with all of that in mind, is there really a limit to the amount of willpower you have each day? I recently went through the book, *The Willpower Instinct*, written by *Dr. Kelly McGonigal* (no relation to Professor McGonagall that I'm aware of). In the book Kelly presents research and countless case studies that clearly show that we do indeed have a limit to our daily willpower.

Imagine that your willpower is like a bottle of water. Each morning you start with the bottle filled to the top. And each time you make a decision or have to use willpower, such as deciding to get up instead of hitting snooze on the alarm clock, a little of the water gets poured out. As you go through your day you'll eventually "pour out" all of your stored-up willpower.

When the willpower well runs dry

So, what happens when the willpower well runs dry? Typically, it leads to poor behavior, such as:

- Procrastination
- Making bad decisions
- Poor performance

If you find yourself experiencing these types of thought patterns, it could very well be due to hitting your willpower limit too quickly.

I know from experience that I typically write my best code in the morning when I'm fresh, whereas I find myself running into more development bugs when I work later in the evening. When I realized this pattern, it made me believe even deeper in the concept of willpower limits and how they can negatively affect performance.

Saving up willpower

With all of this in mind, the concept of saving up our willpower reserves seems like a pretty important concept. Let's go back to the water bottle analogy. If you were in a desert and had a limited supply of water, what would you do? I think the obvious answer is that you would only use the water when it was needed.

So, if we treat our willpower like a precious resource, it would make the most sense to use it on our most important tasks each day.

What's a practical way of doing this? Let's walk through a simple but practical example.

One outfit to rule them all

If you watch my show on CronDose you may have noticed something... You get a gold star if you noticed that for the last 13 weeks (14 weeks if you include this week) I've worn the same shirt. Please note, it's not the same exact shirt. When I decided to experiment with the *one outfit* concept I purchased eight identical shirts.

So why am I doing this? By wearing the identical outfit each day, it completely removes the set of decisions that I would normally have to make each morning when I'm getting dressed. I no longer have to pick between 100+ shirt and jeans combinations. And it has the added benefit that it's quite comfortable.

Does wearing the same outfit each day really help improve my performance? I can't scientifically say one way or the other. Most likely it has a negligible effect. However, it has a much more powerful benefit than simply removing my morning outfit decision. Each day when I put this shirt on it reminds me that I have a limit to my willpower and that I need to use it wisely. And having that mindset does make a difference.

Being a copycat

As a side note, the idea of wearing the same outfit is not an original idea. Steve Jobs, President Obama, and Mark Zuckerberg all have a similar ritual and that's where I got the idea from. If some of the most successful individuals in the world make it a priority to remove any and all unnecessary decisions, I thought it would be a good idea to try out.

Focusing willpower

Wearing the same outfit each day is a good idea for taking care of some low-hanging decision-making fruit, but it's only the beginning. To really ensure that you get the most out of your willpower each day, you need to be intentional with how you use it.

For example, I've talked before about how I have a daily list of to-do items that I follow religiously. To ensure that I'm getting the most out of my day, I always schedule my most challenging tasks in the morning. By taking this approach, I don't risk running out of willpower while I'm working on a vital project. From there I save my lower priority to-dos, such as reading, for the end of the day.

By following this pattern, I've noticed a significant improvement in my work over the past few months and I also feel more relaxed at the end of the day.

Summary

I hope that this has been a helpful discussion on the topic of willpower limits and that it has given you some ideas on how to manage your own willpower.

9

Cramming Versus Consistent Study and a Study System that Works

In this chapter, I'm going to discuss the concept of cramming versus consistent study. And don't change the channel if you're not in school, if you're a developer, or if you want to learn software development the learning never ends.

On an average, I typically go through over a dozen books at the same time and around 4-5 various online courses because the deeper I get into development, the more I realize how much more I really need to understand.

With that in mind, I think the topic of cramming versus consistent study habits should be beneficial since the way that we study is just as important as the volume of how much we study. Most of us have been in the situation where we put off studying for too long and before we know it an exam is upon us that we have to cram for. If you can remember back to the last time that you crammed for an exam or project, how much of what you studied can you remember today?

If you're like me, probably not much. While I was in college I was very bad at this and ended up cramming for many of my midterms and finals, with mixed results from a grade perspective. However, once I got to computer science graduate school at Texas Tech I ran into a problem—cramming didn't work at all.

Software development concepts build upon themselves, so what was taught in the Fall semester would be the foundation for even more complex topics that would be discussed in the Spring. In the Fall, I would learn about logic programming and in the Spring, I'd have a course where I had to build a production application using the Prolog programming language.

Using cramming as a study technique resulted in me having very poor retention of what I was learning, which meant I had to go back and relearn the topics that I had already forgotten from the previous semester. I don't have to tell you how stressful this made my academic life, not to mention the fact that I was working as a full-time developer at the same time. So, I knew that something had to change and I put together a system for helping me retain what I learned each day through a consistent study pattern. Much like a function in programming, my system for consistent study takes in a few parameters:

- Scheduling
- Fighting procrastination

For scheduling I created a to-do list, segmented by day, for what I needed to study, which included academic papers, books, and watching online lectures. I put these in a drag and drop to-do list on Basecamp. After I studied a particular item I would drag it up to the next day's to-do list so I would have a visual cue that I was done for that day.

For me, I would procrastinate studying because staring at the list of the books I had to read was intimidating, and this was mainly due to the fact that I didn't set any practical goals for studying. If you stare at a Discrete Mathematics textbook and tell yourself to study, it's natural to want to put it off; however, if you set small goals, you're less likely to put it off.

With that in mind, I'll put a note, such as read 3 pages of my Information Retrieval textbook, and 3 pages doesn't sound nearly as scary as the vague "just study" mindset. The interesting result in making small, manageable goals for studying is that not only does it help curb procrastination, but typically I will also read much more than the 3 pages. There have been plenty of times where I set of goal of a few pages of a book and ended up reading a few chapters.

With all this being said, there are times where I plan deep work study sessions. In one of these sessions I will set aside 2-3 hours of time to sit down, without distractions, and work through a complex topic. However, I always limit the time to no more than 2-3 hours per day, and I will usually not study any other topics on these days since I'm usually mentally drained by the end of them.

Chapter 9

I hope that this chapter has been helpful and will help you develop your own system for studying so that you can retain when you learn and be able to use it when it matters most.

10
Is Reading Important for Developers?

Throughout this book, I have written quite a bit about improving as a developer, specifically discussing various ways to study from a practical perspective. However, in this chapter, I want to specifically answer the question: *is reading important for developers?*

The short answer to the question is: yes! However, as computer scientists it's poor form to simply take someone at their word. So, let's dive into why reading is critical to improvement.

Why is reading important for developers?

Let's analyze a few key statistics with regard to reading.

CEOs and reading

How many books do you currently read a year? If your answer is that you're too busy to read entire books, let me ask you another question: are you busier than the CEOs of the world's most successful companies? Probably not.

However, research from the Rype Academy (`http://rypeapp.com/blog/5-easy-ways-to-read-more-books-and-double-your-knowledge/`) shows that CEOs such as Elon Musk, Mark Cuban, and Peter Thiel read around 60 books a year! That's 4-5 books each month.

Compounded learning

So why do some of the most successful individuals in the world take the time to go through so many books? At a high level it may seem excessive, but if you truly believe that knowledge is power, wouldn't it make sense to dedicate whatever time is needed to attain more knowledge?

If you look at reading like a form of linear learning, then yes, reading would be a waste of time. Linear learning would be a 1 to 1 transfer of knowledge. For example, if it took the author of the book 10 years to research a topic and it took me 10 years to go through the book, that would be pretty pointless. At the end of the day this type of reading would be pointless.

However, I look at reading like it's compounded learning. What is compounded learning? Good question! Compounded learning is the process of taking the knowledge from an individual, but not having to spend the same amount of time that it took that individual to research the topic.

A compounded learning case study

For example, imagine that you read a book on *How to Become a Better Developer*. The author of the book had to spend years researching the topic (assuming that it was a well-written/well-researched book). However, if you go through the book in a few weeks, that means that you were able to gain years worth of knowledge in a few weeks!

Research (`http://blogs.plos.org/neurotribes/2011/06/02/` `practical-tips-on-writing-a-book-from-22-brilliant-` `authors/`) shows that top authors will spend a minimum of two years researching a book. And that research time doesn't take into account the fact that authors draw on their entire lifespans to write a book. All of this means that each time you read a book it's as if you were able to gain a lifetime's worth of experiences and wisdom from the author.

The CEO who didn't have time to read

A few years back, I was offered a CTO position for a startup in New York City. The job had a good salary, great stock options, and an excellent product.

However, during a dinner meeting with their Founder/CEO, I asked him about a book I had finished reading that discussed best practices for tech startups. He said that he had never heard of the book.

This wasn't a problem, there are millions of books and I don't judge someone for having different literary tastes than myself. However, the CEO followed this statement up by saying that he didn't have time for reading. He was too busy building the business.

The CEO's view of reading resonated with me during the job consideration process. And I ended up turning down the job. If the CEO didn't dedicate time to read and learn from others, that means that he would be relying solely on his own knowledge and life experiences. And even the most brilliant business person will fail if they think that they already have all the right answers.

Chapter 10

My reading system

It's one thing to say that reading is important; it's another thing entirely to go through a large number of books on a regular basis. With that in mind I've developed my own reading system. This system also takes into account a number of complaints that I've heard others say about reading.

The reading schedule

First and foremost, I schedule a set amount of time each day for reading. Usually, this equals around 1-2 hours; however, on weekends this number can be double that number. At any given point of time, I'm usually going through a dozen books ranging from mind/skill hacking through technical programming books.

Audio books are books too!

I'm not sure where the stigma of audio books came from. However, with my travel schedule, I've discovered that audio books are an invaluable tool in my learning arsenal. Obviously, you can't go through programming books via Audible. However, you can go through skill and business-based books. And I personally have hundreds of books in my Audible account, many of which I've gone through multiple times. In fact, many of the books I've discussed and quoted from were books I listened to rather than read.

Books are too expensive

One of the top complaints I hear from students is that books are too expensive. My response is always: if you're not willing to sacrifice to improve, then you're not going to attain your goals. And that includes sacrificing financially.

With that being said, there are ways that you can go through a large number of books, even if you're on a budget. To start off, your local library has countless books that you can learn from each day. And assuming that you bring the books back on time, a library is a completely free option. I have a library within walking distance of my home in Scottsdale, AZ, and I will visit it a few times a week to discover new books.

Additionally, you can sign up for book memberships. Safari Books Online offers an *All You Can Read* package. I have this membership and have gone through a large number of technical programming books in their database over the years.

Summary

In summary, is reading important for developers? I believe that it is. Reading enables you to activate compounded learning. And if you have the chance to gain years' worth of knowledge and experiences in a few weeks, it seems insane to pass up on an opportunity like that.

11
Learning How to Code – Getting Past Skill Plateaus

A common pattern I see with students learning how to code is:

1. Quickly learning a massive amount of information.
2. Then running into a seemingly insurmountable wall. In this phase, the student typically feels like they've reached the zenith of what they're going to be able to accomplish about development.

This second phase is called a plateau. In this chapter, we're going to walk through strategies for getting past skill plateaus.

It's important to understand that everyone follows a similar pattern when it comes to learning a new skill. This means that you will experience times where it seems like every day you're soaking in a wealth of new information. But it also means that you will run into times where it feels like your mind will limit you from learning anything new.

What is a learning plateau?

When it comes to hitting a learning plateau, it's important to look at the potential root causes for why it's occurring. It's been my experience that no two plateaus are the same. And until you've diagnosed why you're not learning, you won't be able to move on to your next level of skill.

False ceiling

Before I continue I want to reiterate something: *you will never reach a point where your level of skill is maxed out.* Maybe if you're a professional athlete and getting older, then your body is naturally going to decrease in performance. But when it comes to concepts such as understanding development, if you continue to dedicate yourself and if you're willing to listen to experts, your skill will never reach a peak.

Getting past skill plateaus

Over the years I have witnessed a few key reasons why individuals (and myself) run into skill plateaus.

Proper information/resources

When a student lacks access to proper information, it makes learning a more arduous process. Imagine a talented developer in high school who had been relying on her teacher (who had limited skill). In cases like this, the student will need to find additional resources, such as online courses, that will help teach her concepts she's never been taught before.

Best practices

During a phase of the learning cycle when best practices are the focus, students may feel like they are hitting a learning plateau. I remember when I was first learning about test-driven development. The concept seemed counterintuitive. I would spend 2-3 times the amount of time on a feature. And this became incredibly frustrating. It felt like I wasn't learning anything new because my new knowledge wasn't affecting anything on the screen.

However, this phase isn't actually a skill plateau. There are many times where developers need to take a step back and focus on quality over quantity when it comes to building applications.

My advice for going through this phase is to embrace it. Be patient. As soon as you have a firm understanding of how the best practices can be utilized, you'll be able to move onto learning new concepts. The only difference is that now you will be able to leverage your new skills, the result being that you'll be a more refined developer.

Chapter 11

Challenging/new tasks

In my experience, the main cause of students hitting a skill plateau is when they stop challenging themselves. If you remember back to when you were first learning development, it seemed like your knowledge was skyrocketing each day.

The reason for this was because each of the concepts you were learning were completely new to you. However, after a certain period of time it seems like it's natural for us to want to become comfortable. Instead of trying to learn something new each day, we simply try to duplicate the work that we've done up to a certain point.

This approach is less taxing mentally. However, it has the nasty side effect of limiting how we improve. Whenever I feel like I'm getting into a rut, I will look at popular websites and I'll start to put together a list of features that I want to learn how to build. From that point, I can put a plan together for what concepts I need to learn in order to implement them.

Frustration = skill

One of my favorite illustrations of getting past skill plateaus was made by the calligrapher, Jamin Brown:

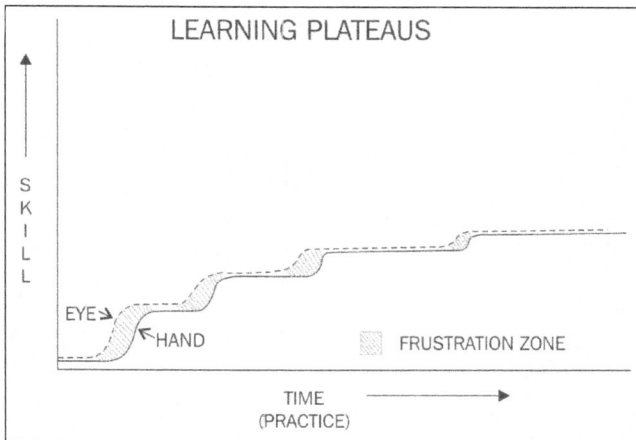

Notice in this illustration how the learning process is filled with plateaus? This is a natural component when it comes to improving at any skill.

But also notice that the key to overcoming a plateau is called the **Frustration Zone**. I think that's a great name for it. Learning complex topics is not easy. As you've probably heard countless times, "if it were easy, everyone would do it".

Becoming a developer can be one of the most rewarding experiences that someone can have. And part of what makes learning how to code so fulfilling is how many challenges you'll need to overcome to succeed.

Summary

I hope that this has been a helpful guide and that you now have some practical strategies for getting past skill plateaus. And good luck with the coding.

12

Developer Learning Curve – Why Learning How to Code Takes So Long

When it comes to becoming a developer, one of the questions I get asked the most is: why does it take so long to learn how to code? I've discovered the answer can be found in research related to learning curves.

What is the learning curve?

The concept of learning curves has been around since 1885. Typically, the research has been performed in the psychological and cognitive sciences. However, the concept can be clearly utilized when it comes to learning development.

The developer learning curve

The following graph shows the standard learning curve. This was generated by a big data analysis algorithm that analyzed the learning patterns of individuals in a number of industries. The curve is smooth because it takes the average learning process and averages the process.

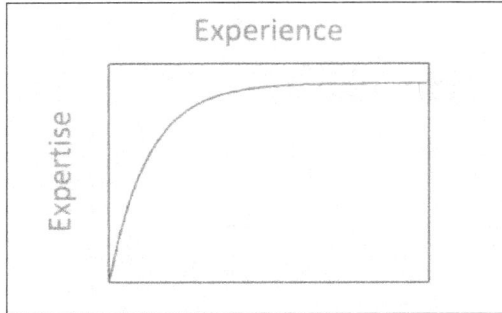

Later in this chapter, we'll take a look at what a learning curve looks like for a single person. Over the years I've had the privilege of teaching students how to become developers. I've witnessed this learning curve play out again and again. And in this chapter, I want to examine the three stages that all developers go through. Additionally, I'll discuss about how long it takes to traverse from one stage to another. The three stages that I'll discuss are:

- Liftoff
- The twilight zone
- The zone

Liftoff

Let's start off by taking a look at the liftoff stage. This is an exciting time for new students. During this time students are immersed in learning skills that they've never seen before:

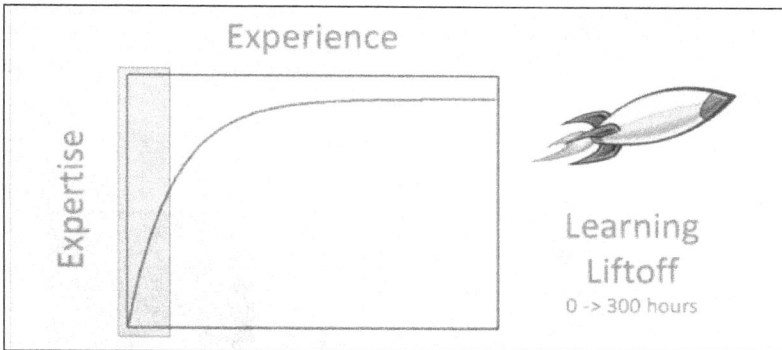

Because all the topics that students learn during this stage are new, their expertise skyrockets. I like to call this the liftoff stage because it's easy to visualize a new student's expertise like a rocket ship soaring into the sky into places it has never been before. During this time, a student will learn how to:

- Configure a development machine
- Learn a programming language
- Work with various frameworks
- Build functional applications

This stage usually lasts for the first 250-300 hours that a developer is learning how to code. This estimate is based on what I've seen with the DevCamp bootcamp students and equals around 6-8 weeks of intensive learning.

As fun as this stage is, it has drawbacks. One of the key problems is that it can give students false confidence. When they see themselves building applications that actually work, it's natural to believe that they can dive right into building production apps for clients. However, they don't realize that they're about to enter… the twilight zone of learning how to code.

The twilight zone

After the exciting liftoff stage of the developer learning curve, aspiring developers will enter the twilight zone:

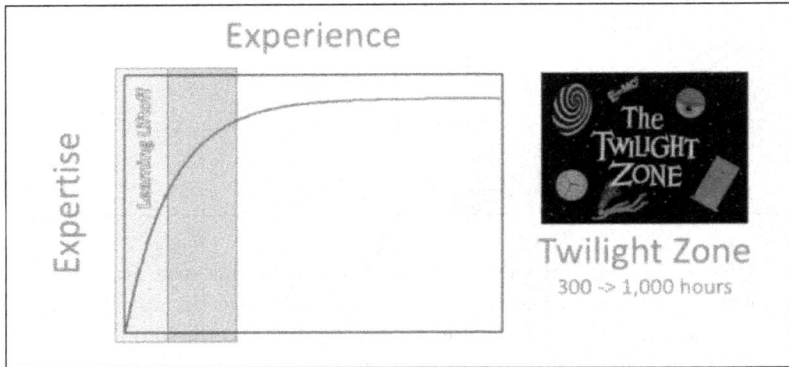

This is a challenging time for students and many students decide to quit programming entirely during this stage.

So why is this time so challenging? After seeing countless students go through it, I've discovered that there are a number of contributing factors:

- While in this stage, many of the core concepts and commands haven't cemented themselves in a student's long-term memory. This results in them having to constantly look up documentation, query Stack Overflow, and things like that.
- During this time, the novelty of simply having an application work has worn off. Now students are asked to perform advanced tasks such as:
  - Working with legacy applications
  - Debugging defects
  - Improving performance
  - Building features that they don't have a step-by-step tutorial for

- Additionally, while working through the twilight zone, students are expected to start implementing best practices. In the launch stage, the primary goal was to get applications functional.

During this next phase, students start learning how to build applications that can be used in real-world scenarios. This means that a student may spend five times longer to build an application with the identical feature of something they created during the launch stage.

This can be frustrating; however, the increased time spent implementing best practices allow the applications to be scalable and flexible enough to be used in production. This is in stark contrast to the apps created during the launch phase that don't adhere to industry standards.

The zone

There is good news though; if a student persists through the twilight zone of learning they will enter The Zone of the developer learning curve:

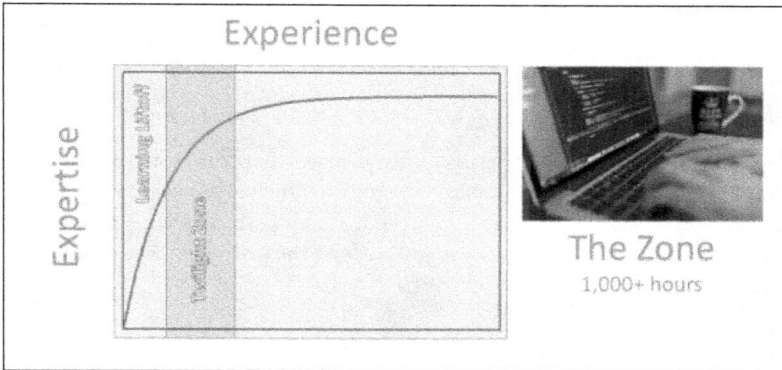

This zone is entered usually after around 1,000 hours of study and work. During this stage, developers have a wide range of features they can build without having to look up the documentation.

In this stage, when you visit Stack Overflow you'll be answering as many questions as you ask. And thankfully, learning new concepts will come easier. The reason why learning is easier at this stage is because you will have developed a mental model of development.

For example, I recently started working with the Scala programming language. I've been able to pick up on how to build applications in Scala dramatically faster than when I started learning C or PHP a decade ago. This is because I have a decade of knowledge in the development space that allows me to frame the new concepts. When I read the documentation and see what it says about data types, I don't have to wonder what a data type is. Instead I can skip ahead to learning the syntax.

As you'll notice in the developer learning curve, the growth pattern in this phase is less than the other two stages. As you've heard me say countless times, learning never ends for developers. However, learning does change. During this phase, a developer focuses on learning topics such as:

- Incremental performance improvements
- Building helper code libraries
- Refining how application code flows

A unique journey

Throughout this chapter you may have noticed that the developer learning curve was smooth. However, that's not reality. The reason why the curve was smooth was because it averaged out the learning path of a large number of individuals. When it comes to a single student, the learning curve looks more like the following graph:

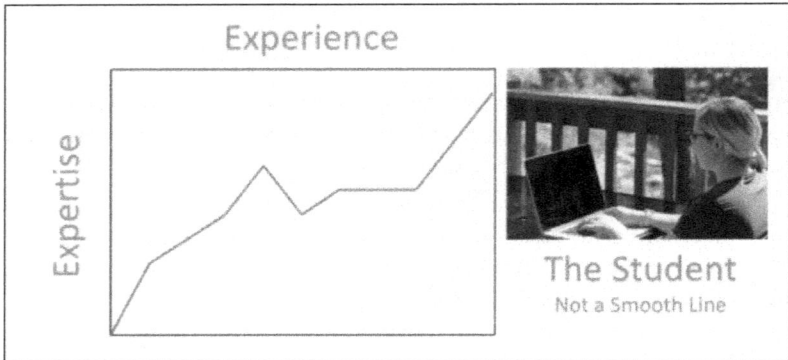

There are ups and downs throughout the learning cycle. As a student, you may decide to switch programming languages after a few years (like I did when I switched from PHP to Ruby around 5 years ago).

Even though you don't have to start back from scratch, it will still take time to learn a new language or framework. And throughout your development journey you'll discover plenty of ups and downs. So, don't get discouraged if you aren't satisfied with your skill level, because I have a secret to tell you: good developers never feel like they've arrived and are done learning.

Summary

I hope that this has been a helpful guide to understanding the developer learning curve, and good luck with the coding.

13

Slowing Down to Learn How to Code Faster

Nowadays, it seems like everyone wants to do things faster. We want to pay without taking out a credit card or cash. Social media lets us share images and videos from our lives in a split second. And we get frustrated if Netflix takes more than 3 seconds to start streaming our latest TV show series binge. However, if you want to learn how to code faster, I'm going to present an odd idea: **go slower**.

This may seem like a counterintuitive concept. After all, don't coding bootcamps, even DevCamp where I teach, tell you how you can learn how to code in a few months? Well yes, and research shows that 8 weeks is a powerful number when it comes to learning. The Navy Seal training program specifically chose 8 weeks as its timeframe for conditioning candidates. And if you search the web for the phrase 8 Week Training programs, you'll find courses ranging from running 10ks to speaking Spanish fluently.

So yes, I'm huge believer that individuals can learn an incredible amount of information in a short period of time. But what I'm talking about here is becoming more deliberate when it comes to learning new information.

Learn how to code faster

If you're like me, when you learn a new topic the first thing you'll do is either move onto the next topic or repeat the concept as quickly as humanly possible. For example, when I learn a new Ruby or Scala programming method I'll usually jump right into using it in as many different situations as possible. However, I've discovered that this may not be the best approach because it's very short-sighted.

Our default mind

When it comes to learning how to code, one of the most challenging requirements is moving knowledge from our short-term memory to our long-term memory.

Remember the last time you learned a programming technique. Do you remember how easy it felt when you repeated what the instructor taught? The syntax seemed straightforward and it probably seemed like there was no way you would forget how to implement the feature. But after a few days, if you try to rebuild the component, is it easy or hard?

If you're like me, the concept that seemed incredibly easy only a few days ago now causes you to draw a blank. But don't worry. This doesn't mean that we're incompetent. Instead, it means that this piece of knowledge wasn't given the chance to move from our short-term to our long-term memory.

Hacking the mind

So, if our default mindset is to forget what we've learned after a few days (or a few minutes), how can we learn anything? This is where our brain's default programming comes into play and where we can hack the way that we learn.

I'm currently teaching myself the TypeScript programming language. TypeScript is the language that is recommended for Angular 2 development, so I thought it would be a good next language to learn. However, instead of taking my default approach, which is to slam through training guides and tutorials, I'm taking a more methodical approach.

Slowing it down

Through my learning path, I'm going through a number of books and video series. And as I follow along with the guides, as soon as I learn a new topic I completely stop. I'll stand up. Write the new component on one of my whiteboards. And actually, write the program out by hand.

After that, I type the program out on the keyboard... very slowly. So slowly that I know I could go around 4-5x faster. But by taking this approach I'm forcing my mind to think about the new concept instead of rushing through it. When it comes to working with our long-term memory, this approach is more effective than simply flying through a concept because it forces our minds to think through each keystroke.

Chapter 13

Bend it like Beethoven

I didn't learn this technique from another developer. Instead, I heard about how one of the most successful classical music institutions in the world, the Meadowmount School of Music in New York, taught students new music compositions. As a game, the school gives out portions of the sheet music. So, where most schools will give each student the full song, Meadowmount splits the music up into pieces.

From there, it hands each student a single piece for them to focus on. From that point, the student will only learn to place that single piece of music. They will start out very slowly. They won't rush through notes because they don't even know how they fit into the song. This approach teaches them how to concentrate on learning a new song one note at a time.

From that point, the students trade note cards and then focus on learning another piece of the song. They continue with trading cards until each student has been able to work through the entire set of cards.

By forcing the students to break a song into pieces they no longer will have any weak points in a song. Instead, the students will have focused on the notes themselves. From this point, it's trivial for all the students in the class to combine their knowledge and learn how to play the song all the way through.

From classical music to coding

So, can this approach help you learn how to code faster? I think so. The research shows that by slowing down and breaking concepts into small pieces, it's easier for students to transfer information from the short-term to long-term memory.

A practical system

So, the next time you are learning a coding concept, take a step back. Instead of simply copying what the instructor is teaching, write it down on a piece of paper. Walk through exactly what is happening in a program.

If you take this approach, you will discover that you're not longer simply following a teacher's set of steps, but that you'll actually learn how the concepts work. And if you get to the stage of understanding, you will be ready to transfer that knowledge to your long-term memory and remember it for good.

14

Mental Models for Learning How to Code and Improve as a Developer

I've talked quite a bit about what it takes to become a great developer. To achieve a level of mastery, I've discussed a number of criteria and in this chapter, I want to add a new pre-requisite to the list.

Let me begin by asking you a question. If I showed you some code, would you be able to tell me in a few seconds if it's good or not? The world of software development is incredibly complex. However, I've discovered over the years that the best developers have the uncanny ability to instantly judge the quality of someone's code.

I spoke to you in *Chapter 2, Are Developers Born or Made? – Debunking the Myth of Prodigies* about the notion that prodigies and savants are a myth. But if this is the case, how can expert developers analyze programs so quickly? To answer this question, we need to go back to Fake Ancient Greece.

Mental models for the Kouros

I said Fake Ancient Greece because my favorite illustration of mental models was discovered alongside one of the greatest forgeries in modern art history.

In Malcolm Gladwell's book *Blink*, he tells the story of the Greek Kouros. In 1985, the Getty Museum purchased a Greek statue called the Kouros for over $9 million dollars. Initially, the museum was hesitant to purchase the statue because there was a significant fear that sculpture was a fake. Kouros pieces were so incredibly rare, the chances that a legitimate and well cared for piece had been discovered were slim to none.

However, the museum was willing to take the risk and embarked on a fact-finding mission. They put the statue through every scientific test available at the time. And the Kouros passed with flying colors. After going through the full examination, the museum purchased the Kouros for $9 million dollars.

Art historians from all over the world were flown in for the unveiling of the Kouros. But something went terribly wrong. The moment that these specialists saw the statue they knew the Kouros was a fake. Interestingly enough they couldn't give any actual reason.

They simply knew that something was not quite right. Their suspicions turned out to be correct and the Kouros ended up being proved to be a hoax. But how were these individuals able to do what countless scientific studies could not? It all comes down to mental models.

What are mental models?

In preparation for this chapter, I was discussing the topic of mental models with a friend and was surprised when she looked at me, confused. After informing me that she'd never heard of mental models, I decided to add this section to explain what mental models are. And after that we'll get into how we can build them to learn development.

A mental model is a mental representation of a specific topic or skill. You can't create a mental model overnight or with cram sessions. Mental models are developed through years of repetition and countless hours of honing a craft.

My Dad is a major league hitting coach for the Houston Astros. Throughout my life I've been able to watch him instruct hitters on how they can improve their swings.

Chapter 14

And I'll never stop being amazed by the fact that he can watch a new hitter's swing and within a split second pick out multiple ways that the player can improve. I can tell you that he did not develop this skill in a short period of time. He has spent more time watching hitters and film than anyone I know. And over the years he has developed a mental model of what the perfect swing looks like.

Mental models for developers

OK, so we've talked about art historians and baseball coaches, but how can we create mental models as developers? You may or may not like the answer, but it doesn't really matter because it's the truth. Mental models are made through repetition.

However, repetition by itself isn't enough. For example, if you built an identical program every day for 10 years you would get really, really good at building that one application. However, you wouldn't improve as a developer. I've talked before how medical research shows that doctors who have spent years practicing on the same types of patient are less proficient than doctors fresh out of residency. In the same way, as developers we improve when we're stretching ourselves each day.

You can stretch yourself by doing things such as:

* Learning a new programming language or framework
* Teaching others how to learn programming
* Creating an open source code library and allowing other developers to use it

Einstein said it best when he said:

"The only source of knowledge is experience."

Summary

If you dedicate enough time each day improving yourself as a developer, you will be able to truthfully answer yes to the question I posed at the start of this chapter. You will be able to have the ability to look at a piece of code and instantly know if it's good or bad. And you'll know that it's not some type of coding super power; instead, it's a skill that you earned through your constant pursuit of improving as a developer.

15

A Developer's Guide for Hacking Procrastination to Achieve Success

There you are. Sitting in front of your computer. Staring at a blank screen. You know you have to work on a code project, but it feels like you're frozen. The task before you is so intimidating that you don't even know where you begin. It feels as if you'd rather be doing anything else in the world besides that task that's staring you in the face.

This scenario is the ugly and all-too-common face of procrastination that programmers are forced to fight constantly. If this situation sounds familiar, you're in good company. But if you want to become a professional developer, you'll need to implement a system for **hacking procrastination**. And that's what we're going to walk through in this chapter.

As the lead instructor for DevCamp I get asked questions from students from around the world. However, one of the most prevalent inquiries I get from aspiring coders is how to overcome procrastination.

Root causes of procrastination

Before we walk through a system for hacking procrastination, we first need to dive into the root causes for this negative habit. Everyone is unique, but over the years I've seen procrastination is typically caused by three thought patterns:

- Perfectionism
- Fear of success
- Lack of planning

To overcome procrastination and get back on track we'll need to address each one of these issues. Because if you let any of these mindsets control the way your mind operates, you will never be able to reach your potential.

Hacking procrastination

I called this chapter hacking procrastination because I think that **hacking** is the most appropriate term for what needs to happen to achieve success. Developers hack applications to build features or fix bugs. In the same way, we need to hack our thought patterns so that our brains function properly.

Before we go through the system I want to make one concept clear. As humans, we were made for action. Procrastination is a negative habit that we've learned through fear-driven thought patterns. To be successful at anything in life, whether it's development or business, overcoming procrastination is a requirement.

Hacking perfectionism

Starting off the list of the causes for procrastination is perfectionism. Have you ever watched a baby trying to stand up for the first time? Babies, who haven't learned that failure is a bad thing, will spend countless hours trying to stand up.

Each time they fall down it doesn't seem to faze them in the slightest. But you won't find a baby that lets perfectionism get in the way of achieving their goal. Instead, they will keep trying until they can stand up and eventually walk by themselves.

However, somewhere between the time that we're babies and adults we develop the thought pattern that we're not supposed to fail. So instead of trying and failing until we succeed, we simply try to only perform tasks that we know we can do properly. To hack perfectionism, we have to remove the component in our brain that is afraid of failing.

If you are a developer learning how to build a new feature that you've never worked through before? Let me clear something up. You are going to do it wrong the first time!

And that's 100% fine. If you think that by waiting you are magically going to learn how to perform the task perfectly, you are sadly mistaken. So, step one is: embrace failure and remove the requirement of perfectionism.

Chapter 15

Hacking the fear of success

Next on the list is hacking the fear of success. If you're overcome the trap of perfectionism, congratulations. However, I've seen just as many developers get stuck due to the fear of success as the fear of failure.

This concept may seem odd since success doesn't seem like something that you should be scared of. However, I remember when I was first learning development. When I was walking through a coding book I would get so excited when I discovered a new concept. However, then I would freeze. My mind's first response was:

"If you learn this, then what are you going to do?"

For example, when I first learned how to build a connection to a database, I put the book down and didn't pick it up until weeks later. By learning the database concept, it opened up a new and scary new world of all of the new topics I had to learn after that. All of a sudden, I had to understand:

- SQL queries
- How to build relationships between database tables
- SQL injection requirements
- And the list seemingly went on infinitely in my mind

To hack the fear of success, we need to quieten our minds. The fear of success is really rooted in the fear of the unknown. So, whenever you're feeling this fear, simply take a step back. Be happy that you have learned a new topic. And then move onto the next feature or topic.

Don't let your mind run wild with all of the potential, unknown concepts that you'll need to learn in the future. Like learning anything else, you need to take it one step at a time.

Hacking the plan

Last on the list for hacking procrastination is creating a practical plan. When I recognize that I'm procrastinating I now tell myself to look at my plan of attack. Usually I'll discover that my plan is too general.

For example, if I'm building a payroll application, I may have an item on my to-do list that says: **Build reporting engine**. That's a scary feature! That's the type of item that will stick on my to-do list for weeks without me taking any action.

To fix this, I've learned that if I break the requirement into a series of very small tasks I can break the cycle of procrastination. For the reporting engine feature I can create a series of much smaller, more manageable tasks, such as:

- Create a page for users to access reports
- Implement a database query for pulling the reports from the database
- Build a file downloader for reports

When I break a large and scary feature down into small pieces, I instantly feel better. The feature is no longer scary and I no longer feel like putting it off until tomorrow. Instead, I am able to simply follow a set of small tasks each day until the feature is complete.

Summary

I hope that this has been a helpful guide for helping you break the cycle of procrastination in your own projects and that you will be able to use it to become a more effective developer. I'll leave you with a quote from the book *The Five Elements of Effective Thinking* by *Edward B. Burger* and *Michael Starbird*:

"Being willing to fail is a liberating attribute of transformative thinking."

So, put yourself out there, create a practical plan, and stop procrastinating and start coding!

16
The Problem with Procrastination for Developers

Libraries could be filled to overflowing with books filled on procrastination. Through my life and career, I have gone through self-help books that attempt to explain why people procrastinate along with supplying strategies to help curb procrastination.

And as great as all those books are, no one has been able to describe the true problem with procrastination better in my mind than *Steven Pressfield* in his book *The War of Art*.

The problem with procrastination

In *The War of Art*, Pressfield compares procrastination with being an alcoholic. If you're like me, when I first heard this comparison I was skeptical. I had a hard time connecting myself pushing off writing a blog post until tomorrow with an alcoholic passed out on the sidewalk in front of a bar.

However, I chose to continue reading. Pressfield gave procrastination a name, calling it the resistance. And that was something I could relate to. Whenever I come across a challenging task, it's as if there is a constant voice in my head saying:

> *"Wouldn't this feel great to push to tomorrow?*
> *You'll be excited to do it tomorrow."*

And when I give into the voice, it's as if I took a shot of happy pills. I instantly feels as through a weight has been lifted off my shoulders and I feel happy. However, when tomorrow rolls around I've discovered something... the voice comes right back and it's still encouraging me to push the task off again.

Instant gratification

After going through this cycle of procrastination for years I finally did recognize the pattern. And Pressfield was right, procrastinating on tasks has the same root cause as being an alcoholic. Alcoholics are willing to trade long-term joy for short-term happiness. By this I mean that an alcoholic will risk their health, career, and family, all for the sake of the feeling that a drink will give them at that moment.

This pattern is played out in the mind of all of us when we procrastinate. When we continually put off tasks for tomorrow, we are trading long-term success for short-term convenience.

Baby steps to knock out procrastination

I've already presented my system for hacking procrastination. However, I don't want to describe a problem without giving a solution. Therefore, I will conclude by saying that the best way I've discovered to fight procrastination is by taking baby steps.

In his book *Mini Habits, Stephen Guise* made the concept of performing one push up a day famous. Guise was a self-proclaimed procrastinator who despised going to the gym or working out. However, one day he decided he was going to create the mini goal for himself to perform a single push up every single day. By following this approach, he realized that the idea of working out was no longer a scary concept. And therefore wasn't something to procrastinate.

Of course, doing one push up a day would have limited health benefits. But what Guise discovered was that after performing the push up he was usually in the mood for doing more pushups. And eventually, his daily habit morphed into a full daily fitness regime.

Chapter 16

Baby coding steps

I've discovered the same approach works with learning and development. When there is a task that I feel like pushing off, I tell myself that I only have to work on it for thirty minutes.

By giving myself a doable goal, the task is far less intimidating and therefore, I don't feel the same resistance and desire to push it off. And typically, I'll discover that I want to work longer than 30 minutes on the task. The end result being that I get much more done and I no longer fear my daily to-do list.

17
Practical Ways to Use the Pomodoro Technique as a Developer

As we continue to work through ways to hack the developer's mind, the focus of this chapter is going to be on increasing productivity. Specifically, we're going to analyze practical ways to use the Pomodoro Technique.

I'm constantly researching new ways to improve my personal productivity. And through my journey as a developer, a popular approach that I've discovered is the Pomodoro Technique. This is a process that I've utilized and I credit it with allowing me to focus on a large number of tasks each day.

Don't let the weird name scare you away. The Pomodoro Technique is a dead simple productivity system that focuses on splitting tasks into timed intervals throughout the day.

Practical ways to use the Pomodoro Technique

One of the greatest strengths of the Pomodoro Technique is how easy it is to implement. The process that I follow is:

1. Each morning I pick out the tasks that I want to accomplish that day.

2. I then decide how long each task will take. The Pomodoro Technique works on point system. Each time you work through a 25-minute task you earn a point.

3. Typically, I try to earn 10 Pomodoro points each day. This means that if I have 3 tasks that I know will take an hour each, I will earn 6 points for those tasks. And it means that I have 4 additional 25-minute slots available for the rest of the day.

Taking a break

Did you notice how I kept saying 25-minute time slots? There is a reason for the odd number. The Pomodoro Technique places a high priority on taking scheduled breaks. After completing each 25-minute task, you take a 5-minute break. During this free time, you can do anything you want. You can get on social media, you can take a walk around the block, or anything that you want to do. Just make sure that your break does not exceed 5 minutes.

Also, after you've completed 4 tasks it's recommended that you take a 15-minute break. However, you can tailor your breaks and intervals to what works best with your schedule. By planning breaks throughout the day, you will decrease your chances of burn out. And I've noticed that I no longer feel bad about doing things such as checking my Instagram account or Hacker News throughout the day, because I can fit my guilty pleasures into my scheduled free time.

This is one of the aspects that I truly love about the Pomodoro Technique. Many of the other productivity systems I've tried in the past tend to lead individuals towards burning out. However, the Pomodoro approach allows you to have a sense of balance.

Lifestyle versus fads

Have you ever tried dieting before? When I was younger I struggled with my weight and to help fix it, I tried a number of intense diets. This included nutrition strategies such as dramatically decreasing calories, or killing off carbs. However, I noticed that I'd stay true to the diet for a few weeks or even a few months, but eventually I would fall back into poor eating habits.

Once I recognized this trend I moved to having a balanced approach to eating. I stopped trying nutritional fads and I transitioned my focus into eating in a way I felt I could eat for the rest of my life.

I made this change in my nutritional approach a few years ago and it's completely stopped my roller coaster dieting and weight loss and weight gain.

Chapter 17

A lifestyle of productivity

In the same way when I was younger I fell into the same pattern with working on tasks. I'd get excited about working on a project or learning a new programming language. And I would spend countless hours working on what I wanted to accomplish.

However, this approach inevitably led to burning out and large stretches of time where I didn't want to work at all. I look at the Pomodoro Technique in the same way that I look at having a balanced diet. By limiting the number of tasks that I work on each day and by implementing planned breaks between each task, I no longer burn myself out.

Additionally, after I have finished my work for the day and have earned my 10 Pomodoro points, I feel a sense of accomplishment that I never felt before. And after work, I don't feel guilty spending time with my family and friends, because I know that I completed every task that I set out to work on that day.

Practical implementation

So how can you implement the program? There are a few ways. To start off, you can simply use the timer on your phone and then count up each of the tasks/points that you achieved each day. That's how I started off working with the Pomodoro Technique.

Additionally, there are a number of smartphone apps that have Pomodoro timers and even allow for creating a task list that you can use as a pick list for your tasks each day. I like these types of apps because they also give you historical analytics so you can see how many tasks you've completed each day. The Pomodoro focus app (`https://itunes.apple.com/us/app/pomodoro-time-focus-timer/id973134470?mt=12`) is my personal favorite (and it's free).

18

The Power of Making Mistakes – Learning by Failing

Let's take a step back in time back to my first semester of Computer Science grad school. Stepping into my first class I was filled with nervous excitement. The class was taught by Dr. Gelfond, one of the most respected individuals in the artificial intelligence sector.

As class progressed I witnessed a disturbing trend. Instead of simply lecturing us like our other professors, Dr. Gelfond constantly called students up front to write programs on the chalkboard or to describe a concept he discussed. This wouldn't be a big deal, except that he made a habit of calling us up front specifically when it was clear that we did not understand the concept. Was he cruel? Did he want to make us look ignorant in front of the entire class?

The secret weapon to mastery – making mistakes

Actually, the opposite was true. Instead, Dr. Gelfond cared enough about us that he imparted to us the secret weapon to mastery: making mistakes. Wait, making mistakes is the opposite of what our mind tells us to do, right? Making mistakes is embarrassing. Mistakes tell the world that we don't understand a concept. However, making mistakes also provides a number of powerful tools that anyone interested in learning should be aware of.

Making mistakes – memory steroids

First and foremost, when you make mistakes, especially publicly, you're going to feel like you're taking memory steroids. How so? When I think back to Dr. Gelfond's class I still remember every mistake I made when I was called in front of the class. The memories generated by making mistakes are so vivid that they can be recalled, even years later like mine. Now obviously simply remembering the mistakes by themselves would be pointless.

However, in addition to remembering what I did wrong, more importantly I remember what I had to do to correct my mistake. It's been over three years since I took that class, but I can still remember each of the key concepts that he taught us. And I can tell you from experience that I cannot say the same thing about all of the classes I've taken.

Mistakes force learning

Another benefit to making mistakes is that they force you to learn. No one likes being wrong. So, assuming that you have a passion for knowledge, you can use the memory of making mistakes to help motivate you to learn a concept properly.

If Dr. Gelfond would have simply stood in front of the class and lectured for the entire semester, I most likely would have studied enough to do well on the tests and leave it at that. However, because I constantly had the thought in the back of my mind that I may have to be called up in front of the class to write a program or describe a concept, it forced me to study harder than I would have for a test. This healthy fear took me from simply being able to remember a concept to truly mastering it.

Mistakes kill pride

Lastly, making mistakes helps to kill pride. Proverbs 16:18 says:

"Pride goes before destruction, a haughty spirit before a fall."

One of the largest obstacles to learning is pride. Anyone puffed up with pride will find that their learning progress will come to a halt. When someone is filled with pride they can't see beyond their own limited knowledge. Thankfully, if you embrace the process of learning by making mistakes, pride will never be able to stake a claim in you. By their very nature mistakes force you to realize that you don't know everything, and that you have more to learn… which we all do.

Chapter 18

Summary

So, whether you are just learning to code from scratch or if you're a seasoned developer, never be afraid to make mistakes. Mistakes reveal that you're traversing into new territory that you've never been before, which is what you need to do to go from mediocrity to mastery.

19

Learn How to Code – The Guide to Memorization

During a recent bootcamp teaching session where I was walking through a number of frontend development techniques, a student asked a great question. Referencing the CSS styles, she asked:

"What is the best way to remember all of the specific style names and properties?"

This is a vital question to answer, especially for new students. For example, if you look at the CSS documentation you'll find thousands of potential style options. If you're learning these styles for the first time that list can be pretty intimidating. And that doesn't even bring in the idea of learning how the styles work together with applications as a whole!

Obviously, this issue does not only apply to CSS styles. When it comes to learning development, whether it's a programming language or framework, you will be greeted with a large amount of information that you'll need to memorize, or at least know where to reference it.

The guide to memorization

At first glance, this may seem like a daunting task. And many aspiring developers have given up on their learning journey because it seems like an insurmountable challenge.

However, I'm here to tell you that it's completely realistic for you to learn how to work with a large number of complex concepts. And if you follow the system I outline in this chapter, you'll be amazed at how quickly you pick up on memorizing more information than you ever thought possible.

Repetition

Before I go into the memorization system I have used over the years, it's important to say that repetition is the key to memorizing large amounts of information. None of the techniques I will give you are going to help if you don't take the time to work through them consistently.

Smarter, not harder

With that being said, it's important to know that, by itself, repetition is a slow and naive memory training technique. As a development student, imagine that I had a list of a few hundred method names and tell you to memorize them. If you were to simply stare at the sheet of paper and try to memorize the names, how do you think you'd do? If you're like me and the majority of the world, probably not very well.

The reason why dry repetition isn't a great way to memorize names is because it doesn't give you a frame of reference for the names.

Visual mental mapping

In the first memory technique, we're going to walk through visual mental mapping. Our minds are incredible at memorization. However, at the same time, our minds are also picky with how they store information. Let's run a quick test. If I show you 15 random digits, such as:

- 234
- 348532
- 984
- 234523
- 34534
- 35234
- 234
- 25345
- 234
- 985
- 553
- 37434

- 740
- 423
- 9812

And I give you 5 seconds to look at each number. How many of the numbers will you repeat back to me? Unless your name is Dustin Hoffman, you probably won't be able to name very many!

However, what if I showed you the pictures of 15 celebrities? Now if I give you the same test as with the numbers, do you think you'd do a better job remembering the list of celebrities or the random numbers? Assuming you know who the celebrities are, you'd be able to repeat back a significantly larger number of celebrities than numbers.

The reason for this difference is because you have a frame of reference for the celebrities and in this exercise, you had a visual reference. By combining these two things your brain was fully prepared to recite back a larger number of items from the second list.

With this knowledge in mind we can apply the same principles for memorizing anything.

Short-term versus long-term memory

Because our brains are efficient machines they naturally sort information based on priority. You are most likely aware that you have short-term and long-term memory. This concept is the reason why you can instantly remember your second-grade teacher's name decades later, but may forget a new acquaintance's name 30 seconds after hearing it.

Typically, the brain doesn't log knowledge into our long-term memory bank unless it thinks we're going to need it in the future. This is kind of like how a computer works. If you add text to a document and save the file on the hard drive, that's like storing information in the mind's long-term memory.

However, if you run a calculation in the terminal the computer processes the information in memory and then discards it, which is like how our short-term memory system works.

Implementing visual mental mapping

So, when it comes to implementing the visual mental mapping technique, we're essentially tricking our brain into thinking that it needs to move a piece of information into long-term memory. In this process, we associate a visual image with the term that we want to memorize. A key prerequisite for this to work is that the visualization needs to be relevant to the term (or the behavior of the term).

Getting back to the developer's initial question. Let's see how we can use visual mental mapping to memorize a CSS style. I'm going to use the `text-decoration` property as a case study. In the world of CSS, the `text-decoration` element allows you to add or remove an underline style to a piece of text. With this in mind, I would create an image in my mind that would look something like this:

So, in this example I have an image filled with decorations. And on top of the image, I have some text that is underlined. And it's sitting on the decorated fireplace mantle. By creating this visual image, I've mapped:

- Decoration to underlined text
- A familiar image to something abstract

And with this mental image in place, I don't have to think about the term `text-decoration`, instead I will think of a decorated fireplace with underlined text sitting on the mantle. This visual is much easier for my brain to accept into long term memory because it has a direct frame of reference.

The text-decoration word is no longer a foreign element trying to invade my memory. Instead, it's catching a ride on an image that already has a home in my long-term memory.

Taking a real-world example

Sticking with our celebrity theme. Imagine that you wanted to go to a private, VIP party in Hollywood. If you just try to show up the bouncer at the door most likely won't let you in. However, if you're friends with Brad Pitt and you walk in together, you won't have any issues attending the party.

Visual mental mapping follows the same principle. Our brains guard our long-term memory to ensure that our mind doesn't get cluttered with useless information. For example, what if you logged every piece of information that you come across each day into your long-term memory?

As you drive down the street to work your brain captures millions of data points, such as street signs and people walking, etc. If your brain didn't guard against useless information entering your long-term memory bank, all of this information would be treated with the same priority as your parent's names. Obviously, this wouldn't be a good idea!

So, our brains are like the guard in the VIP Hollywood party. And when we attach a new piece of information to something already logged in long term memory, it's like we're having Brad Pitt escort us into the party.

Finding patterns

So visual mental mapping seems like a great idea. However, the idea of creating thousands of visualizations isn't very practical, which is why, when I'm learning a new programming language, I also focus on picking up on patterns.

Returning to our case study of memorizing CSS elements, let's take a look at the border attributes available in CSS3:

- `border`
- `border-bottom`
- `border-bottom-color`
- `border-bottom-style`
- `border-bottom-width`
- `border-color`
- `border-left`
- `border-left-color`
- `border-left-style`
- `border-left-width`
- `border-radius`
- `border-right`
- `border-right-color`
- `border-right-style`

- `border-right-width`
- `border-style`
- `border-top`
- `border-top-color`
- `border-top-style`
- `border-top-width`
- `border-width`

As you can see, there are 21 available attributes. And that's just for managing border styles on a webpage! As you can imagine, it would be pretty intimidating to memorize this list, especially when you realize that it's only a very small percentage of the available CSS styles needed for development.

However, if you start to analyze the list you'll notice a number of trends. For example, there are a number of styles that simply reference: `top`, `bottom`, `left`, and `right`. These styles are simply ways for giving a border style to a specific side of an element.

Additionally, you may also notice that each side also has a set of options for color, style, and width. So practically, if you know that these elements are all available to the border set of elements, this list can be shrunk down to 5 items:

- border
- border-color
- border-radius
- border-style
- border-width

This is more manageable.

Copy and paste is the enemy

In addition to creating visual mental maps and using patterns, I'm going to finish off the list of memorization techniques with the recommendation to not copy and paste new concepts that you're trying to learn.

I first heard this advice from *Zed A. Shaw*, the author of the *Learn Hard* programming book series. He instructs his readers to not even look at the book at the same time that they're implementing the code. He postulates that by forcing yourself to type in the code without referencing the documentation while typing, it forces the mind to actually think through each keystroke.

In my personal experience as a developer and with teaching, I've discovered a significant difference between the students that copied and pasted code or simply followed along with a tutorial, compared with the students that attempted (even unsuccessfully) to implement the code by themselves.

Not everything has to be memorized

On a final note, I want to dispel a common fallacy. As a developer, you don't have to memorize every class and method to build a project.

Even professional programmers constantly look up documentation on a regular basis. Instead of feeling like you have to memorize everything, focus on memorizing the terms that you use the most. This will make the memorization process more practical and natural.

20

A System for Learning a New Programming Language

In this chapter, I'm going to discuss how to learn a new programming language. I'll walk you through the five steps that I use whenever I'm learning a new language or framework.

Over the years, I've been hired by organizations such as Learn.co and AppDev to write programming curriculums for:

- Ruby on Rails
- Ruby programming
- Python
- Java
- Several JavaScript frameworks

The only language that I really build applications in is Ruby, which means that I've been forced to become proficient in a number of language that I really didn't have much experience working with, sometimes in a very short period of time. And over the years I've developed a system for learning a new language or framework, and that's what I'm going to walk through in this chapter.

When I'm learning a new programming language I follow these steps:

1. Watch a full tutorial series on the language. When I'm watching I don't try to follow along, I simply watch what the instructor does in the demos so I can get a high-level view of the language syntax and flow.

2. Create a *hello world* application. I'll incorporate a few basics, such as **running a loop, creating and instantiating a class,** and any other high-level concepts I remember from the tutorial.

3. Pick out a sorting algorithm and implement it in the language. It's fine if the sorting algorithm is a basic one such as selection or bubble sort. Sorting algorithms force you to use data structures, loops, variables, and functions. Combining each of these elements will give you a good handle on how the language works.

4. Go through an advanced tutorial on the language and this time follow along and build the programs with the instructor.

5. Go through coding interview questions for the language. Being able to confidently answer these questions will give you a good idea if you have a solid understanding of the language.

I've used these five steps for a number of languages and I can also tell you, once you've become proficient in a single language you'll find it's much easier to pick up new programming languages since most of them have quite a bit of shared processes, and all you'll need to do is learn the difference in syntax.

I hope these tips will help you learn a new programming language. Please feel free to write to me with any other methods that you've found helpful when learning, and good luck with the coding!

21

Development Study Tips – Reverse Note-Taking

In this chapter, we're going to go back in time and walk through when I developed the system of reverse note-taking. A quick Google search will show that I have coined the term; however, I did not invent the process.

Back when I started computer science grad school at Texas Tech I was struggling with one of my classes. It had been about a decade since I had been in a classroom environment and I was having a difficult time paying attention to the 1.5-hour lectures.

The problem with traditional note-taking

During this time, I spent quite a bit of time meeting with Dr. Richard Watson. And during one of our meetings I brought up the issues I was having. His first question was based around how I was taking notes for the course.

I showed him my notes and he instantly told me that I was taking notes completely wrong. He pointed out multiple places in my notes where I had missed key concepts that were unifying elements. And without noting these items, I wouldn't understand the topics at all.

In reviewing the notes, I realized he was completely right. I spent my time writing down facts and what I thought were key terms. However, I regularly failed to articulate how everything worked together.

For example, for my notes on tree data structures I outlined each of the key elements of binary search trees and B-Trees. But I failed to describe the innate differences between the tree components from a behavior perspective.

This is similar to taking notes in a history class and writing down the names, dates, and locations for Napoleon's loss at the battle of Waterloo without describing the critical differences between his old armies with the one he lost with.

Reverse note-taking

Finding out that I was taking notes wrong was great. But it wouldn't have been too useful without learning an alternative approach. So, Dr. Watson asked me to try a different type of note-taking technique.

He said to put my pen and paper away during class. And instead of taking notes during class, he recommended that I simply listen to the lecture. He instructed that as soon as the lecture was over I should find a quiet place and *then* write down all the topics that I remembered from the discussion.

Initially, I was skeptical of this approach, mainly because I was afraid that the important concepts would go in one ear and out the other. He added that I should tape record the lecture so that I could use the recording as a safety net for the topics that I failed to remember.

Despite my negative perspective on the approach, I decided to give it a try. (Obviously, my natural note-taking approach wasn't effective, so I didn't have much to lose). I followed Dr. Watson's advice to the letter. And I was pleasantly surprised to discover that I remembered much more information using this reverse note-taking approach compared with simply trying to write down concepts during the lecture.

Benefits of reverse note-taking

I started following this reverse note-taking process years ago and I still use it today. Through this time, I've noticed a number of key benefits to this approach.

Narrowed focus

First and foremost, by having the knowledge that I will have to recite back the key components of the lecture forces me to have an increased level of focus. This is opposite to how I used to take notes. My old way of taking notes would many times distract me from the concepts being discussed. I would hear a concept that I felt was important and I would take my focus away from the speaker and focus on writing down the topic.

Many times, this would inadvertently result steal my focus away from another important concept, or a description of how the topic I was writing down worked at a high level.

Chapter 21

Additionally, as a naturally competitive person I would make a game of how much I could remember from each lecture. If I could remember enough to write down two pages of notes on Monday, I would try to write down two and a half pages on Tuesday. By making a game of the practice it forced me to narrow my focus even more on the content.

Story-based mindset

Another benefit of reverse note-taking is that it forced me to think of the lecture as a unified story instead of a series of facts. Let's go back to our illustration of Napoleon's battle at Waterloo. If you listen to a lecture about the battle and take notes during the class, you'd probably do things like write down the following:

- General names
- Cities where battles took place
- Dates

However, if you simply listen intently to the lecture and recite it back afterwards you won't repeat dates and locations. Instead you will naturally remember the battle in story form. You'll discuss the struggles that the Duke of Wellington had to overcome to lead the charge against the French army. And because it's a story, your retention of the topics will be considerably higher compared with attempting to memorize facts and figures.

If I were to ask you to remember a high school history class and a movie you saw in high school, would you have a better chance of remembering the plot of the movie or the history lecture?

So, getting back to my computer science grad school experience, by leveraging the reverse note-taking strategy I forced myself to think of the topics discussed during the lecture as a story as opposed to a bunch of theories and math equations.

Forced repetition

Lastly, the reverse note-taking approach made it easier to review the lecture material compared with my old style of note-taking. Before that I would rarely listen to a lecture recording. Even if I had the intention to listen to the recording, other priorities always seemed to override the task. I mainly attribute this failure to the fact that I, for some reason, trusted my notes.

However, when I started reverse note-taking I would always listen to the lecture a second time to fill in any items that I missed during my post note-writing session. I discovered this single benefit to be critical to my success since it became an automatic habit to reinforce my knowledge. In contrast to my old approach where I trusted my untrustworthy notes, with reverse note-taking I didn't trust my memory, so I knew I had to reinforce my memory. And the consequence was that I always would listen to a lecture twice, with the final result being a dramatic increase in retention.

Summary

This approach is not for everyone. I know students who excel with a more traditional note-taking strategy. However, if you find yourself in a situation like mine, I highly recommend you giving reverse note-taking a chance. You may be surprised how effective it can be.

Part 2

Freelancer Skills

22

Tips for Organically Growing a Freelance Business

I strongly recommend that you think about freelance techniques whether you're a freelance developer today or you are working with freelancers in some capacity. You'll gain insights into thinking and coding, whatever type of developer you are today.

Your career will be smarter if you're able to think—at least when it's a help—like a successful freelance developer. That's what this part of this guide is all about: thinking smartly and for yourself as a developer!

We'll begin by discussing how to organically grow a freelance business as a developer. When I say organically, I mean that these are strategies that should work while you sleep. For example, I have had some of my largest clients contact me out of the blue based on them coming across a blog post or GitHub project I published.

Organically growing a freelance business

Having an organic marketing strategy is key for building a sustainable business. And in my experience the marketing mechanisms that have been the most effective are the six I will discuss.

Referral requests

Starting off the list are referral requests. Word of mouth marketing is one of the most powerful tools you can use for acquiring new clients. Imagine a real-world scenario of referrals. If someone opens up a new restaurant in your town, are you more likely to be influenced by the restaurant advertisements or one of your close friends telling you how great the food was?

If you're like me, if a friend sings the praises of the restaurant I'm going to, I value their opinion much more than an ad from the restaurant itself. The reason for this is because I trust my friend more than the restaurant. It works the same way when it comes to marketing yourself as a freelancer. If you have happy clients they can help grow your business.

Over the years I've had multiple clients refer their friends and colleagues to me. However, I've also discovered that sometimes it helps to give them a little push. After you have successfully completed a project is a great time to ask a client if they have any friends that may need your services.

Blogging

Next on the list of organic marketing strategies is blogging. I considered placing blogging at the top of the list because it's such a powerful tool. Over the years I have been contacted by multiple clients that told me they found me via my blog and subsequently hired me.

Blogging is content marketing at its finest. With your blog, you can showcase your skills, position yourself as an expert in the field, and give clients a taste of your personality. If you have never blogged before and are wondering what type of content to write, here are some high-level topics that have worked for me:

- *Tutorials showing how to build features I specialize in.* For example, if you focus on building eCommerce websites, you could write blog posts explaining how to connect an application to a payment gateway.
- *Soft-skill strategies.* For this you can write posts related to experiences you have had while learning how to become a freelancer. An example could be writing about a time when you had a challenging client and how you were able to work with them effectively. These types of posts have multiple benefits since they are effective for content marketing and allow you to contribute to the freelancer community.

Chapter 22

Expert positioning

Blogging is a great way to position yourself as an expert. However, writing blog posts is not the only way to be considered an expert. Another great way to accomplish this feat is to contribute to other blogs and news outlets.

If you look at my personal site you'll see that I've been interviewed or quoted in dozens of blogs and magazines over the years. These outlets include sites such as ReadWriteWeb and the magazine CIO.

And don't worry, you don't have to pay a high-priced PR firm to be quoted on these types of sites. I personally use a service called HARO (https://www.helpareporter.com/), which stands for Help A Reporter Out. HARO pairs individuals with reporters around the world. The way it works is that reporters can post requests on HARO asking for interviews or quotes on a topic they are researching. Each day I monitor HARO and when I see a topic that I am familiar with I'll write up a few sentences and send them to the reporter.

Don't let the expert moniker scare you away. There are many times where I am far from an expert in a field that I've been quoted in. However, I'll perform a little time researching a reporter's question and then I'll simply give my opinion. This type of marketing is great because:

- It's free
- Credible reporters are the ones positioning you as an expert
- Many times, the reporter will link back to your website, which helps from an SEO perspective

Open source contribution

Next on the list of strategies for organically growing a freelance business is contributing to the open source community. When it comes to open source contributions, there are a number of strategies that you can take:

- **Direct code contribution**: This usually comes in the form of creating a code library that other developers can use. One of the more successful Rails development firms in the world, thoughtbot, has taken this approach to the extreme. The thoughtbot team has built libraries such as FactoryGirl, Paperclip, and Administrate.

  These Ruby gems are some of the most popular gems in the Ruby development ecosystem and the thoughtbot team released these libraries completely for free. However, I can assure you that the company's open source contributions are directly related to acquiring clients.

- **Tutorials**: If you don't feel that you're quite ready for building a code library that other developers will use, that's perfectly fine. You can find a feature that you feel comfortable developing and you can create a screencast in which you walk through your process for building the component.
- **Contributing to pre-existing libraries**: Another great way to contribute to the open source community is to help add features or fix bugs on pre-existing code libraries. You can easily discover the full list of requested features for a code library by looking at its issue list on GitHub. By taking this approach, you don't have to worry about building a code library from scratch. You can simply add onto another app, which helps the original development team and will give you experience and confidence in working with professional code bases. Personally, I contributed to multiple Eventbrite API RubyGems and built-in functionality that previously didn't exist.

Social media marketing

No guide that discusses organically growing a freelance business would be complete without mentioning social media marketing. I have to admit that this is probably my least favorite marketing channel. If you peruse Twitter, Facebook, or Instagram it seems like they are cluttered with annoying sales pitches.

However, I have been discovered by multiple clients via my social media accounts. Each day I try to post a development picture on Instagram. And by taking this approach, I have received a number of unsolicited project requests. And several of these requests have turned into freelance clients.

When it comes to social media marketing my recommendation is to find an outlet that you enjoy working with. And once you've picked your favorite channel, put all of your available energy into that specific service.

This is important, because if you pick out an outlet that you don't like, you're not going to want to post on it in a regular basis. And when it comes to social media marketing, consistency is key to success.

Summary

In summary, when it comes to organically growing a freelance business I focus on three approaches. First, once you have happy clients, work on getting them to refer you to their friends and colleagues. Next, make sure that you're constantly blogging and positioning yourself as an expert in your space. And lastly, find a social media outlet that you enjoy working in and post on it daily.

23

Freelancing Tips – Knowing When to Fire a Client

If you're starting on your freelance journey, or still even considering it, the topic of this chapter may seem insane. However, I can ensure you that knowing when to fire a client is a critical component of building a successful freelance business. It can also sharpen up the same decision-making skills you use every day as a developer in general.

My urgent client

A few years ago, I was hired by a fast-rising startup. The company had skyrocketing growth, and I was hired to build their platform. After going through the interview process, I was hired. Soon after taking the client, I met with a developer who was leaving the organization.

After the developer walked me through the system he gave me a word of warning. He mentioned that the CEO of the company had a favorite word: **urgent**. I filed the information in the back of my mind and started working on the application. Within days, I learned why the previous developer left the fast-growing startup. Literally EVERY email the CEO sent me contained the word urgent in some form or another.

Through the course of around a year I worked with the company and built out the full system. However, I noticed that my quality of life was negatively affected by this single client. My nights and weekends were no longer filled with spending time with my family. Instead that time was spent working through countless urgent tasks from the client.

When to fire a client

After a while it dawned on me that if I continued to work with this client, I was actually losing the benefits of being a freelancer. Being a freelancer is supposed to result in freedom and making my own schedule, right?

Once I realized that this client was making my life worse instead of better, I put a plan in place and told him that I would no longer be working with him. Through that experience I developed a system for deciding when to fire a client. There are three criteria that have to be met, and I've listed them here.

#1 – being treated like an employee

First on the list for deciding when to fire a client is when you are treated like an employee. Being treated like an employee typically means that you're expected to be on the company's schedule and thus limit your own freedom/flexibility. I have had multiple times where a client appeared to forget that I was a freelancer. Some telltale signs of this happening are:

- *When a client is frustrated that they can't communicate with you 24/7.* I once had a client that I had to fire because their employees would send me Skype messages all day and night for trivial issues. And then they would be frustrated if I didn't respond immediately.
- *No organized communication.* Over the years, I've had clients who would let multiple employees message or call me any time they needed a task completed. It's important to have a set number of project stakeholders. If a client lets any/all employees send you requests it's pretty much guaranteed that communication conflicts will occur.

When I realize that a client is treating me like an employee, I'll approach the CEO or whoever my direct report is, and I'll convey my concerns. Many times, this will fix the issue. However, there have been times where the problem persists and I have been forced to fire the client.

#2 – tyranny of urgent

Returning to my story from the beginning of this chapter, a top reason for knowing when to fire a client is when they can't separate urgent from normal tasks. I remember a time where this specific client set up a project management job board. I kid you not, 90% of the tasks were marked with the tag urgent.

Chapter 23

Not only is this a stressful situation, it is also a recipe for failure. When all tasks are marked as urgent it essentially means that none of them are urgent because there's no designation between the projects.

In the book *Rework*, *Fried* and *Hansson* recommend that companies remove the word urgent from their dictionaries. I highly recommend this approach.

Typically, when a client marks tasks as **urgent** or **ASAP**, it means that they don't know how to properly manage a project. And poor project management skills are not an attribute you want in a client, because a client who doesn't know how to manage a project will eventually blame you for not implementing their plan properly.

#3 – toxic environment

Last on the list for knowing when to fire a client is when it's a toxic environment. I've been fortunate to not run into this situation very often. However, over the years I have a had a few toxic clients. Being toxic can take a number of forms, including:

- Constant negativity
- Poor communication
- Unrealistic deadlines
- Moral/integrity issues

I can think of one client that embodied each of these traits. He hired me to build an application and gave an incredibly vague list of requirements. Throughout the build of the project I would send daily project updates and he would go weeks without giving feedback at all.

When I would hear from him, all his comments were negative. In many of the cases he would be upset for not implementing features that he had never even mentioned in his vague list of features. Needless to say, I fired the client on the spot and moved on to greener pastures.

The joy of firing a client

When I started out as a freelancer the thought of firing a client seemed crazy. However, as I built up my business, I came to the realization that firing a client that constantly brought stress into my life actually resulted in making me a better freelancer.

Toxic clients are not fun to work with. They cause anxiety and kill the joy that freelancing should bring. So, I'm constantly pruning my client list. And the more experienced I get as a freelancer, the better my client list has become. This has resulted in more joy for me and better performance in regard to what I produce for clients.

24

Dodging Silver Bullets for Scalable Freelance Projects

Does the idea of a code library fulfilling a significant portion of a freelance project that you're contracted into, sound appealing? It's OK, you can be honest and say yes, whether you're an active freelance developer today, or will be in the future.

When I started out on my freelance journey, any time I came across a large feature request, the first thing I'd do was check to see if there was a code library that took care of the requirement. In the development world, code libraries like these are called silver bullets.

However, as appealing as it may sound for a plugin or library to take care of the lion's share of a project, it's been my experience that this approach ends up taking longer to implement than simply building the components from scratch.

The problem with silver bullets

Let's start off with a practical case study. A few years ago, I took on a fleet management project. The set of requirements included features such as:

- Having full CRUD capabilities for a number of database tables
- Creating a search engine that could search through various attributes of each database table
- The ability to use filters to drill down data
- And a number of other items related to a reporting dashboard

After starting the project, I started to research code libraries that would work as silver bullets and take care of the key features. After a few days, I came across the RubyGem called rails admin. The rails admin gem is pretty impressive. It includes features such as:

- Easily querying database tables
- Implement custom filters for running advanced queries
- Export records to Excel/CSV
- Add new records from the dashboard
- Edit/delete records

As you may have noticed, this code library looks like it fits nicely with the set of requirements for the project I had.

Silver bullet customization

I quickly went to work building out the application. And I integrated the rails admin gem as a cornerstone component of the project. The client was ecstatic during the demo. They absolutely loved the application and they were shocked I could build the app so quickly.

So, what was the problem? The issues started when the client started to ask for new features. After testing the application out for a few weeks, they came back with feature requests such as:

- Being able to save common queries
- Export out to rare file formats that worked with their accounting system
- Integrate a tax API to calculate depreciation

Each of these new features are relatively common requests for a fleet management system. There was just one problem. Because I built the entire application around the rails admin code library I was limited to the features that the gem offered. And this was a problem because rails admin turned out to be incredibly difficult to modify.

In fact, after several weeks of tedious work, I concluded that it would take less time to build the entire system from scratch as opposed to customize the gem itself. So, the end result was that I wasted quite a bit of time and the project was delayed, all because I thought a single silver bullet code library was going to be able to take care of a significant portion of the application.

Chapter 24

Becoming a sharp shooter with code libraries

So, does this mean that I'm suggesting that you stay away from code libraries entirely? No, not at all! Part of the reason why freelancing is possible (and affordable for clients) is that you don't have to create 100% of an app's functionality from scratch.

Instead, I've learned to be selective about the code libraries that I integrate. Let's look at a couple of the code libraries that I regularly use on projects:

- **Pundit**, for building a permission structure. Pundit is a lightweight code library that is easy to customize and doesn't lock you into a narrow set of permission features.
- **Devise**, for authentication. Writing an authentication system from scratch is time consuming. The Devise gem allows Rails developers to quickly integrate features such as registration, login, logout, and advanced components such as secure password retrieval. Additionally, Devise is customizable and I've rarely run into a situation where it didn't work for an app's requirements.

Do you notice how these code libraries operate like helper libraries for specific features? My rule for integrating code libraries into projects is that I pick out packages that assist with small elements of a project. And I shy away from silver bullets that promise to take care of large portions of a project's functionality, but are difficult to customize.

25

A Freelance Guide to Managing Advanced Features

One issue that every freelancer comes across at some time or another is managing advanced features. And by advanced features I mean that a client asks you to build functionality that you've never built before when this happens to you.

Notice that I said *when* and not *if?* That's because every freelancer, no matter how experienced, has been asked to build something they've never created before.

Managing advanced features

Over the years, I've been asked to build a wide range of features. Some of them I had experience with, and others... not so much. A good example of this was a number of years ago when I was asked to build out a GPS tracking iPhone app. The client wanted to track their employees in the field and allow them to remotely submit tickets. Sounds like a great idea, right? I thought so too. There were just a couple of issues:

- At the time, I hadn't built a single mobile application, much less a production app
- My experience with real-time GPS tracking was minimal

Due to my lack of experience, my first thought was to pass on the project. However, the client was a Fortune 500 company and at the time I did have long-term plans on building out my mobile portfolio. Not to mention that the job paid well over $100,000. With these factors in mind I took the offer.

The talent pool

Now I would have been insane if I thought I could build an application like the one they requested by myself. With zero experience and no domain expertise in mobile apps, the project would have died before it even started. Therefore, as soon as I signed the contract I searched Upwork for a mobile specialist to help build the application.

I found a great iOS developer and we agreed on a mutually beneficial contract where I would manage the client and he would build out the application. This was a foreign concept to me since all the other projects I worked on were ones where I built out 100% of the functionality.

However, if you decide to take on projects that you have limited expertise in, partnering with other developers is a great way to expand into new markets.

The process

The application development process was different than any I had ever experienced before. I was used to working on every component of a client application. However, for this application I limited my work to the web API development. This allowed me to work with the mobile developer on a daily basis and after around six months we completed the project.

As a controlling person, I found the process challenging on a number of levels. The main issue I ran into was due to feature scheduling. Since the mobile developer was remote, I had to work with his schedule. There were a number of times when this caused issues because I would have an API component completed and I had to wait until he completed a mobile feature, and vice versa.

However, after switching to a Kanban project management board we could schedule our tasks in a more organized manner.

Chapter 25

Kanban

To review Kanban boards, remember that they are a project management system where you have a number of columns designated as:

- Pending
- Working
- Under review
- Completed

We organized each of our tasks into each of these columns. And from that point we were both able to see what features needed to be worked on. Being able to see the stage for each component allowed us to move forward in a more organized fashion than when we were working independently.

The result

After a number of sleepless nights and few frustrated back and forth emails we finished the project. And not only was the project a success, the application has processed tens of millions of dollars worth of tickets and is still used to this day by one of the world's largest energy companies.

Summary

So, when a client asks you to build a feature that you have zero experience with, my advice is to partner with a specialist in that area. The example I gave in this chapter was specific to situations where a freelancer has literally no experience building a feature.

There have also been times where I was asked to build a feature I had experience with, but I wasn't comfortable committing to building a production application. In those cases, I hired a mentor to answer questions that I had during the development process, and those projects turned out quite well. And they had the added bonus of teaching me how to build advanced features I had limited experience with.

In summary, when it comes to managing advanced features for clients, don't let your lack of experience stop you from getting jobs. As a freelancer, you have access to a nearly limitless supply of resources to help you build any project.

A caveat

Before you go out and take on a dozen jobs that you have no clue how to build, let me add a word of caution.

I have seen freelancers and even large software development agencies take the approach of believing that they can simply hire outsourcers to do all their work for them. This approach will fail every time.

To work with outside contractors, you need to work with them daily. Did you notice how one of the prerequisites to the mobile application I worked on in this chapter was that I had a clear communication channel with the mobile developer?

If I would have simply sent him a list of requirements and waited for the finished product the project would have failed miserably. Working with contractors is typically just as time consuming as writing the code yourself. So, don't think that outside contractors are a magic bullet that will do all of your work for you.

26

Freelancer Interviews – Practical Tips for Taking Over a Legacy Application

In this chapter, I interview a freelance developer that I have a tremendous amount of respect for, Derek Harrington. In fact, when I decided to launch DevCamp, I had to let go of a number of my freelance clients. And Derek was who I handed the majority of my clients to. Based on my experience with him over the years, I knew he would take great care of the clients and that they would be pleased with his expertise.

In this chapter, I ask Derek a few questions related to freelancing. Specifically, we discuss practical tips for taking over a legacy application.

Derek's tips can of course apply to any developer whether you're a freelancer or not in your current situation – which is why I recommend for any developer to learn from Derek's freelance approach to this common coding situation!

What is the first thing you do when you take over a legacy application?

Write tests. When you identify the pieces of the code that need refactoring, write specs first to cover the functionality of the feature, then refactor the code and ensure your tests still pass.

What other practical tips for taking over a legacy application that have worked for you in the past?

In evaluating a legacy codebase, use the previous developer if you have access to him/her. Lean on them for info. Ask questions like "what would he do differently?", "what bits of code did he really want to refactor but never got around to it?", "what part of the code is he/she the most proud of?". Lean on their experience to help guide your evaluation. Many times, bad legacy code isn't so much the result of an incompetent developer, but of poor project management and deadline-driven developer pressure.

What are your thoughts on refactoring a code base Skill Up: A Software Developer's Guide to Life and Career starting over from scratch?

Resist the need to rewrite everything so it's perfect. We've all inherited some nasty codebases and if we're going to be honest about it, we've all been that culprit more than once in our careers. But don't rewrite for the sake of rewriting. That's irresponsible.

If you're going to re-write from scratch, make sure you're doing it for the right reasons. We all want to work on brand new projects using the most recent versions of every new technology framework. It's much more enjoyable.

Sometimes it's not the best thing for the project and the client though. Make sure your decision is justified by more than "you wanting to do it". Sloppy code can be cleaned up. Tests can be added. Versions can be upgraded. Old code with poor app architecture riddled with brittle, unstable features and a failure to use any general best practices or third-party tools can be a good justification for rewriting. Lack of understanding of a confusing app is not a justifiable reason.

When is the best time to work on fixing poorly written code?

Just like re-writing an application from scratch, it's irresponsible to leave messy code that every developer on the team is going to touch. There's a time to let bad code be. But not when you're tripping it over it every time you work on the app.

27
Five Tips for Taking Over a Legacy Application

Let`s continue discussing the topic of taking over a legacy application. It's one of the dirty little secrets in the freelance world that a high percentage of the projects that you'll be asked to work on are actually legacy applications, which means that you'll be taking over or working with other developers on pre-existing apps.

There have been a number of times where I've had great experiences taking over a legacy application. Notably I was hired a few years ago to work on a legacy app for Eventbrite, and I was very pleased to find a very well configured codebase. It only took me about a week to become familiar with the inner workings of the application, and I could start building new features right away, it was a great experience.

However, that rarely occurs, typically freelancers are taking over a legacy application because the previous developer was fired from the project or due to the app owner having issues with the performance of the software.

As a case in point, a few years ago I was asked to become the lead developer for a legacy Rails application that had been around for a while and already had multiple developers. This was already a bit of a red flag since well-written applications are typically much easier to maintain, and therefore the original developers are usually still around in some fashion or another. And to put it nicely the app code was convoluted and even after a year it was still difficult to add new features. The legacy code was so fragile that one change could have a domino effect and break other features, with a number of the bugs not showing up until weeks later.

Needless to say, the situation was a mess. I was explaining my predicament to a good friend of mine who was a pretty experienced developer, and he recommended I read *Working Effectively with Legacy Code* by *Michael Feathers*. Thankfully, I could take what I learned in that book to help completely revamp the application that I had been having issues with. I'll now share with you the tips and techniques I learned there about taking over legacy projects.

Tips for taking over a legacy application

While there are a number of techniques you need to apply to work with a legacy application, the first should be building a comprehensive test suite.

Creating a test suite

No matter what language or framework that you work in, you will be able to create automated tests that capture the functionality of the application. So, in the legacy application I was working on I started creating tests for each model.

I began with basic unit tests and then started branching out to integration tests that ensured that the various elements of the codebase were communicating properly with each other. Going through this process had the added bonus that I became more familiar with the structure of the app and I could refactor the code as I implemented the tests.

Adding new features via TDD

Once the test suite was built, I started building all new features via the **TDD** (**test-driven development**) method, which ensured that the test suite was up to date. By utilizing this process, it also made it possible to ensure that the new features that I added wouldn't break pre-existing functionality. This is called regression testing.

Breaking out specific features into microservices

The further I got into the codebase, I started to notice that the app had become bloated with features, and many of the components didn't need to be included in the core application.

Chapter 27

Therefore, I slowly started creating microservice applications that handled isolated pieces of functionality. Some examples were: creating a microservice that managed the user notification system and building an app that processed the reporting engine. After creating the microservices, I could get rid of significant portions of the legacy code and then simply wire up the legacy application with the new microservices so they communicated properly.

DRY up the codebase

In many legacy applications, you'll run into duplicate code that causes a number of problems, including the issue of having to make one change in multiple places in the codebase.

An example of this was how the application I was working on dealt with view templates. There were a number of view files with identical HTML code. I could refactor these components into partials that could be shared across the application, which allowed me to make a single code change that would populate throughout the app.

The topic of taking over a legacy application is important to understand, not only for the reason of being prepared for what steps you need to take to work on a legacy app, but also so you will have a better idea of how to build applications from scratch.

Remembering the Eventbrite application that I mentioned earlier, that application was easy to work with and add features to because it had been built from day one using each of the techniques mentioned in this chapter.

If you develop an application from scratch using these best of breed techniques, you will make it easier on yourself when you're adding features in the future. It will have the added benefit that any new developers that may work on the application in the future will be able to start adding new features easily and they'll appreciate the extra work you put into the development process.

Summary

I hope that this has been a helpful guide for taking over a legacy application and that you can apply it on the projects that you're working on.

28
Guide to Freelancing – Starting Over Versus Refactoring

As a freelancer or as part of an organization, you will come across many times where you make a decision on starting over versus refactoring on a legacy project. Over the years I have come across this issue more times than I can count.

The legacy scenario

Typically, the situation sounds something like this. I'll get hired by a client who has a legacy application. The application is usually a few years old and has been managed by a number of developers. I've discovered that usually the code project started out small, and it grew from there.

Somewhere along the way the application lost its way. Instead of using a scalable application design approach, the previous developer patched new features on and the codebase devolved into a convoluted mess. Eventually, every new feature causes another component to break and the client gets so frustrated he decides to hire me.

Does this scenario sound familiar to you at all? As a freelancer, I've been on both sides of the legacy code spectrum. When I was a new developer I built new projects that got out of hand and I lost the clients. And as I matured as a developer I started getting hired to take over legacy projects.

I can tell you from experience that neither side of this scenario are fun, especially when the client brings up the dreaded topic of starting over versus refactoring.

Starting over versus refactoring

When I was a young and naive freelancer I dreaded the idea of re-factoring a legacy application. The second that the client brought up the possibility of starting over from scratch, I jumped on it!

However, the more projects I work on, the more my mindset has changed. Over the years I've put together a system to help me decide between starting over versus refactoring a project. And that's what I'm going to walk through here. The steps I follow are:

1. Removing the fear factor.
2. Analyzing the 80/20 principle.
3. Building an automated bug list.
4. Becoming the client.

#1 – removing the fear factor

One of the reasons why inexperienced freelancers tend to opt for starting a project over is because of fear. And fear is rarely a good reason to make any decision (unless you're running away from a wild animal or something like that). So, before I make a decision, the first task I perform is taking fear out of the equation. I'll ask myself:

"If you weren't afraid of the unknown issues with this codebase, what would your decision be?"

Once fear has been removed I can look at the project from an unbiased viewpoint.

#2 – analyzing the 80/20 principle

The 80/20 principle has a number of practical ramifications. You may have heard it being used to say that 20% of the people make 80% of the wealth. Or that 20% of a customer base generates 80% of a company's revenue. However, I've also seen that the 80/20 principle can work well for deciding between starting over versus refactoring.

Too many times I've seen a freelancer start a project from scratch when the legacy application already contained 80% of the functionality needed from the client. This means that the developer only needed to take care of the remaining 20%.

If you look at the numbers the answer becomes readily apparent. Would you rather perform 100% of the work (which is what would be needed when starting from scratch), or only 20%?

So, in this step I take a step back and I analyze what features the client is asking me to build. If the legacy application is functional and simply has a messy codebase, it's rarely the smart move to start over from scratch. Typically, in this case I'll add the new feature and then start refactoring the application one module at a time.

#3 – building an automated bug list

Moving down my list I'll next use automated tools for analyzing the application. Pretty much every programming language and framework has a wide range of analysis tools. I'll utilize these tools to generate a set of issues for the legacy application. I like this step because it accomplishes two key goals:

1. It gives me a practical strategy for what needs to be fixed in the application.

2. Since it's automated, these types of tools are unbiased. Your personal judgments on the previous developer's coding style are taken out of the equation. And the focus is centered solely around the project itself.

While each project is unique, the tests I run usually focus on giving me a report on:

*   Potential security issues
*   Best practices
*   Code that is not being utilized (this is vital!)

#4 – becoming the client

Lastly, I try my best to remove my personal feelings from the decision. Instead, I focus on taking the perspective of the client. I'll ask myself:

"If I was a fully informed client, would I really want to pay for a developer to start the project over from scratch?"

Using some fuzzy math, I'd estimate that around 9/10 times my answer to this question is that an informed client would request a refactor over starting over. Starting a project over is expensive, and there's no guarantee that the new codebase is going to be perfect.

In fact, I can pretty much guarantee that there will be issues with a brand-new application. I've seen multiple times where a legacy application was replaced by a new piece of software that had the same number of bugs.

When should you start over?

So far, this chapter has heavily favored refactoring an application. However, there are times when starting over from scratch is a better approach. Some of the rationales that make starting over a wise decision for the client are:

- **A complete change in architecture**: I have had clients who requested that I migrate an application from being a monolith (a large single application) to becoming microservice-based (a number of applications that each perform a single feature). In cases like this, it wouldn't make any sense to try to keep the legacy application since the core application structure would have to change.

- **Moving to a different language/framework**: Over the years, I've had a number of clients who had old ASP .NET and PHP applications approach me to rebuild their systems in Ruby. When it comes to changes languages or web frameworks it wouldn't be possible to retain the legacy application.

Notice how both these key reasons had nothing to do with bugs or messy code? The only time I'd recommend for a client to start over from scratch is if it's literally impossible to retain the legacy application.

Summary

In summary, the key to remember is to go through the system of checks whenever you're asked to decide between starting over versus refactoring. The more experienced you get as a developer, the more you'll realize that it's incredibly rare that a functioning legacy application cannot be saved.

29
Should You Use TDD on Freelance Projects? – Comparing Quality Versus Speed

When approaching a new freelance project, one of the first questions many developers and designers ask is:

Do you want it done fast... or properly?

In this chapter, I'm going to specifically discuss if you should use TDD on freelance projects. However, the concepts I'll discuss now apply to any type of quality control system. So, this is great advice for any developer.

Quality versus Speed

There's an old software engineering rule that states that there are three options you have when building a project:

- Quality
- Speed
- Cost

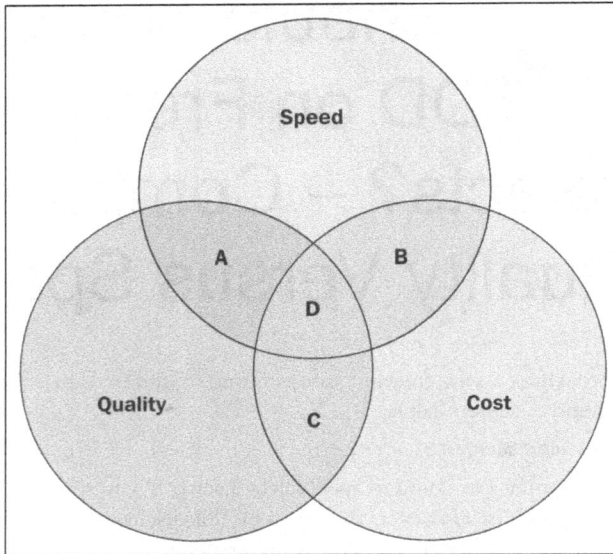

This diagram represents the principle as a Venn diagram. The elusive center is where you have a project that's built quickly, for a low price, and was created with industry-wide best practices. In my experience, it's rare for a project to reside inside of this sweet spot. Instead, I'll tell clients that they can pick two out of the three. For example:

- You can have the project built properly for a low cost, but it's going to take quite a while to develop. This is because the project will need to sit on the back burner since higher paying projects will need to take precedence.
- Alternatively, the project can be built quickly at a low cost. However, this approach won't allow for the time needed to follow best practices, such as building automated tests into the application. I rarely offer this option to clients because it's too tempting for them, and I've seen from experience that these projects always end badly.

Chapter 29

TDD on freelance projects

In this chapter, I've selected the concept of **test-driven development** (**TDD**) as a measurement of project quality for one key reason. Every time that I've been handed a messy legacy project to work on, there is always one common characteristic that they share:

The code doesn't have a comprehensive test suite.

On the other hand, whenever I start working on a high-quality application I've discovered that these projects pretty much always have solid test coverage.

So, I'm not saying that a full test suite is required for a project to be considered a high-quality product. However, in my experience tests seem to be a key indicator that determines how well an application was built.

Making the decision

When you are embarking on a new project how should you decide if you should use TDD?

Giving no choice

I know plenty of developers who simply do not give clients a choice in the matter. All the code that they write will be tested, period and full stop. This helps make the decision process more straightforward. This is the approach I take now, but that's only because I now have the ability to be more picky when it comes to the clients I take on.

However, if you are new to freelancing and you need clients, it can be difficult to tell a client that a project will be around double the time and cost. If you don't have a strong set of pre-existence, you may find yourself in a situation where you price yourself out of the market.

Letting the client decide

Alternatively, you can let the client decide on what approach they want you to take. In this situation, you propose the pros and cons to building a full test suite compared with only building the application itself. If you have an intelligent client they will most likely see the benefits of including tests and choose for the pricier option.

This is an effective strategy because it allows for you to bring the client into the decision-making process, which will make them feel involved in the work. And if the client is still looking at other freelancers, this approach may help win him over.

Another benefit to letting the client decide is that his response may give you insight into how he thinks. If he acts like tests are a pointless luxury and says that he simply cares about getting the project complete, he might be a nightmare client. And in cases like that you are better off moving onto more informed people to work for.

Using common sense

Lastly, make sure that you're using common sense. Imagine being asked to build out a simple corporate website. In cases like this you only need to write some basic tests. At the most this should only add an hour or so to the project.

There is no need to bog down the process writing tests that verify that every CSS class and ID are shown on the page. As with most concepts in freelancing and life, common sense is one of your greatest tools.

30

Automating Client Updates as a Freelance Developer

If you have limited freelancing experience, it may surprise you to discover that a significant portion of a developer's day is spent detailing the work performed for that day. In this chapter, I'm going to walk through automating client updates so that you can be as efficient as possible.

Importance of daily updates

Before diving into how we can automate updates to clients, let's discuss what a proper update is and what it entails. An update is a message sent to a client, usually every day or at least every day that you're working on the client's project. The days are long gone where clients would hire a freelancer and the developer would disappear for a few months until they brought back a finished product.

Nowadays, clients want to have a transparent view of the work performed. This is especially true if a client is paying you on an hourly basis. This makes sense because if you hired someone and paid them for their time, wouldn't you want to know how the time was spent?

Regular and explicit updates are also an important way that you can distinguish yourself from offshore development teams. Over the years I've worked with development teams across the world. And the number one issue I constantly had with them was finding out what they did each day. So, if you can give a transparent view into the work that you perform for a client, it can give you an edge over cheaper, offshore freelancers.

An example of client update

So, what does a good daily update look like? Here is one I took from a real-world client update:

- Integrated CSS fix for the location widget
- Continued working on bug fix for the well on the right side of the page
- Updated CSS for the locations widget on the city pages
- Integrated the checker for posts on the city-specific show pages
- Updated sign up buttons
- Temporarily hide sponsor text
- Implemented changes to the contact us text
- Implemented custom sub division with master division annotation for the forms
- Updated the edit label on the post show view

Notice how these updates are practical and informative. None of the items are too technical, since overly technical updates would simply confuse clients.

Automating client updates

So, we've established that client updates are important and we know what a good client update looks like. However, if we have to type these updates in from scratch every day for multiple clients, it would tally up to quite a bit of time. I'm not a fan of wasting time and I doubt you are either, which poses a dilemma:

1. We need to create a detailed updates of all the work we do each day.
2. But we don't want to waste time writing reports (and isn't our hatred of writing boring reports what made us want to become freelancers in the first place?!).

Whenever I come across a situation like this, I try to see if there is any way that I can automate a boring task. Thankfully there is.

Version control to the rescue

In the beginning, I was writing out all the daily updates manually. However, if I wrote them at the end of the day, I had to go back through all my GitHub commit messages to reference the work that I did.

Chapter 30

After going through this process for a while, it dawned on me that if I simply added a little more detail to my GitHub updates, I could simply copy and paste them each day and I wouldn't have to write them from scratch again.

This process ended up saving me a considerable amount of time each day because for best practice reasons, I had already been writing GitHub commit messages for each new feature I implemented. So, now I can remove the duplicate work I had been doing.

Here is a screenshot of a GitHub project where I used the technique of leveraging commit messages for automating client updates:

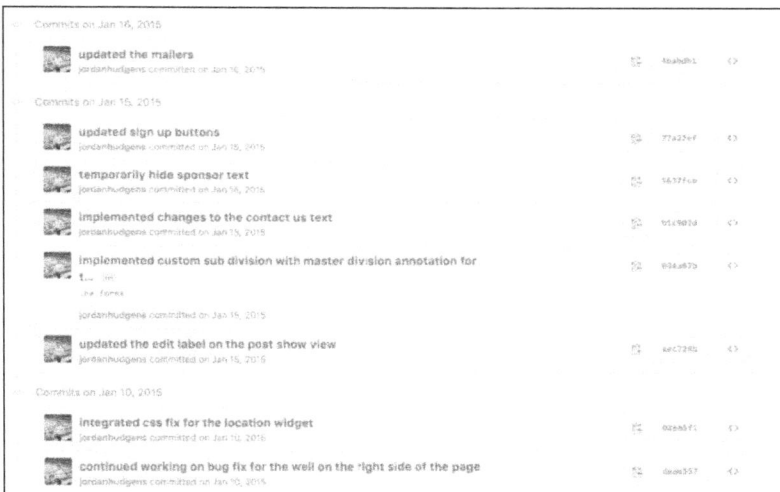

Summary

I hope that this has been a helpful guide for automating client updates, and that you can leverage it with your own clients.

31

Freelance Requirement Elicitation – A Guide for Feature Development

Imagine for a minute that you're a freelance developer who was handed a new feature to build by a client. Then picture yourself building an elegant feature, all the code working perfectly. You follow best practices and ensure that all the potential edge case scenarios are covered.

Now imagine that you're demoing the bright and shiny new feature to the client. But instead of telling you that you're the best developer in the world and they're going to name their first child after you, they look at the application confused, because what you built didn't match what they had in their mind at all.

This is a scenario that is played out all too often in the freelance development world. And in many cases, it's due to a poor requirement elicitation process. The story I just mentioned is not a made-up parable, it happened to me recently. And when I say recently, I mean yesterday (at the time I wrote this).

My Name is Jordan and I Wrote a Poor Requirements Doc… "Hi Jordan…"

So, what did I do wrong? The issue was caused by me rushing through the requirement elicitation phase. I have worked for this specific client for over 5 years and I got lazy confirming the exact set of requirements needed for the feature.

Freelance requirement elicitation

Let's walk through what happened so you can avoid the same embarrassment and wasted time.

How it started

A few weeks ago, the client contacted me and said that an application I built for them needed a new feature. The application is an invoicing system that their drivers utilize to generate invoices for clients:

In an email, the client attached this spreadsheet. He said that the application had to generate this invoice to give to the customer.

The build

After receiving the email, I spent a few days modeling the new feature. I put a list of all the messages that would be passed between modules. I built UML diagrams to ensure the data was modeled properly. After careful planning, I spent two weeks building the new feature and it came out perfectly.

Chapter 31

To be 100% honest, I was very proud of the work that I did. The feature was flawless and completely bug free. It also fit in perfectly with the rest of the application. I deployed the code to the staging server and I waited for the client to start showering me with praise... but the praise never happened.

The problem

I emailed the client and gave a video demo of the feature. A few hours later I received an email from the client that said:

> *I'm confused, what exactly is all of this? In my email, I just meant that we need the invoices to be formatted like this spreadsheet.*

So, it turned out that the client didn't want a new module built into the application at all. Instead, they simply wanted an additional format option for their invoices.

Who was at fault?

So, who exactly was at fault? It may seem natural to put the blame on the client since they didn't make their request clear at all. And I was tempted to get upset and blame them (especially for the first 10-20 seconds of my fury). But then I realized that this issue was completely within my control.

As freelancers, it's our job to manage each stage of a project. If we rush through the requirement elicitation phase, anything that happens after that stage will fall on us.

A better way

So how could this have been avoided? Let's walk through the process I should have followed and that would have led to a better outcome for myself and the client.

Step 1

Right after getting the email I should have responded to the client with clarification questions. Examples might have been:

- *Do you want this to be on a new page of the application?* This is better than saying something like: *Do you want this to be a new module?* Because a nontechnical client isn't going to know what a module is. But they will understand what a new page on the site is.

- *How will this interact with other parts of the website?* This question would have instantly given me the feedback to know that this spreadsheet was simply meant to be a different invoice formatting option.
- *Can you describe the flow of how this will be generated?* This is one of my favorite questions to ask because it forces the client to be explicit with how a new feature should work. Many times, I'll ask a client to create a PowerPoint slide deck showing the flow they want from a feature.

Step 2

After asking clarification questions, I should have followed up with a prototype. I could use a tool such as InVision or even a simple PowerPoint deck where each slide held a different page of the proposed new feature. Examples would be:

- Starting with slide 1, this is where you can click on a button to get to the new page.
- On slide 2 I'd show the form page where the user would enter the information.
- Lastly, on slide 3 I would show the invoice that was generated by the new feature.

A better ending

If I would have followed these two steps, it would have taken me anywhere from few minutes to hours to establish what feature was actually needed. As you can imagine, this is a much better option compared to wasting weeks of development time.

Summary

I hope that this has been a helpful chapter to freelance requirement elicitation and that you'll be able to learn from my mistake and apply it to your own business.

32

How to Remotely Demo Work for Freelance Clients?

So, you have a freelance client and you're ready to show off your work, but how can you showcase a project when you work remotely? If the entire application is completed, you could simply send the client a link to test it out. However, it's been my experience that this approach is not a great idea. As the designer or developer, you know the inner workings of the app.

The client, on the other hand, especially if they're of the non-technical variety, will stumble through testing the application out. Even if you did a great job on the project, if the client doesn't know how to use the software they're not going to be happy with your work.

Why proper demonstrations are important

Over the years, I've discovered that well thought-out demonstrations are a key to successful projects. There are two main reasons for this:

1. A proper demo will let you control the flow of the app. You can control the focus of the work and spend time showcasing how the system works. This will essentially function as a tutorial for the client of the app. A well-organized demo will educate the client on the application and remove many of the common issues related to user experience confusion.

2. You will get practical feedback. No matter how well you think you understood the client requirements, there will always be misunderstandings, especially early in the development process.

Thankfully, if you put together a proper demonstration of the software you can get a clearer view of the client's vision. If you simply sent off a link to the app for the client to test, many of the feedback items they would send back would be related to not understanding how the system functions. However, if you can clearly show how the app works, it will shortcut this process and let you understand the actual fixes sooner.

Review of services to remotely demo work

There are a number of ways that you can remotely demo work for clients. I'm going to go through the processes I've used throughout the past few years and discuss when each option is ideal.

Screencast

The first option I'll review is creating a screencast. This is a great option if there are a number of clients that will need to review the feature:

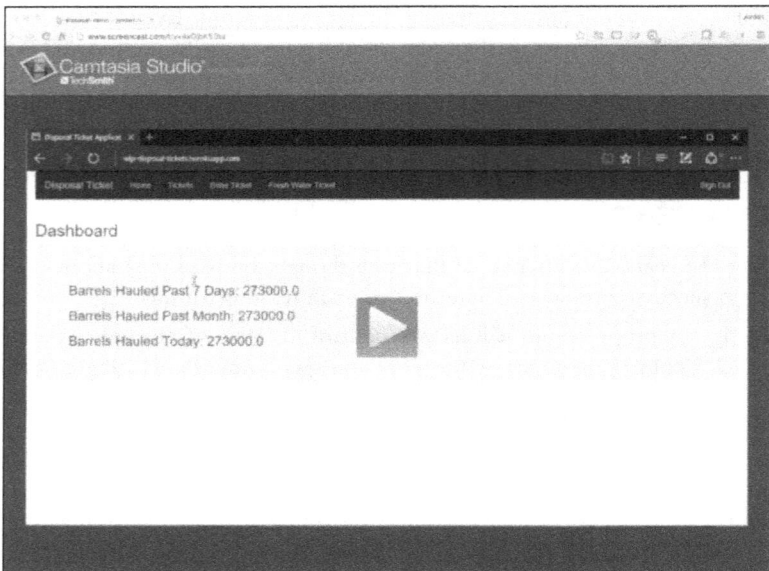

At its core, a screencast is you recording yourself walking through the application. If it's a web-based application, you can have the video showcase each feature of the application. In my own work, I use tools such as:

- Zooming in to specific screen zones
- I highlight sections of the screen that I want to focus on

This process only takes a short period of time. However, it is well worth it because it enables clients to have a tangible walk-through of the system.

You can use a number of tools for recording screencasts. My personal favorite is Camtasia; however, it is a little expensive. So, if you are trying to keep a low budget, there are countless free options, such as Screencast-O-Matic.

After you finish filming a screencast demo, you can upload it to YouTube, Vimeo, or a video hosting site. From there, you can have the client view the link at their convenience.

A remote desktop

Next on the list of tools to remotely demo work is remote desktop sessions. Every client is slightly different. Many clients are fine with email and video demonstrations. However, other clients want more of a personal touch:

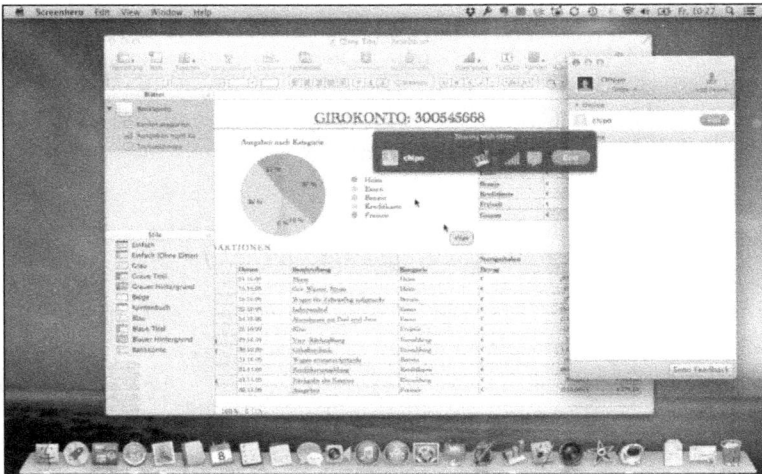

If a client likes to have full interaction with you during the demo, a remote desktop tool may be the best choice for showcasing your work. I have also found that this option is ideal when I'm working for other developers. This is mainly because remote desktop demos allow for pair programming. There are a few different options when it comes to remote desktop tools:

- **GoToMeeting**: If your client wants to have a traditional live demonstration, services such as GoToMeeting or Join.me work nicely. They will let clients view your screen and they also come with dedicated conference call lines if you're working with multiple stakeholders.

- **Screen sharing**: There are times when you need the ability for you and a client to simultaneously walk through a demo. This is for the scenario I just mentioned where you're working for a developer and he wants to be able to go through the app at the same time as you. My favorite service for this type of demo is Screenhero. It offers an easy way to have multiple users control a screen at the same time and it's pretty affordable.

- **Free options**: If you're on a budget, there are a number of free screen sharing and remote desktop options. Some of the notable ones are Google Hangouts, TeamViewer, and Skype.

PowerPoint

Last on the list of tools to remotely demo work are PowerPoint-type presentations. I say type because you don't have to actually use PowerPoint. I've used PowerPoint, Google Slides, and Keynote for product demos. I like using slide-based demos early in the project development process.

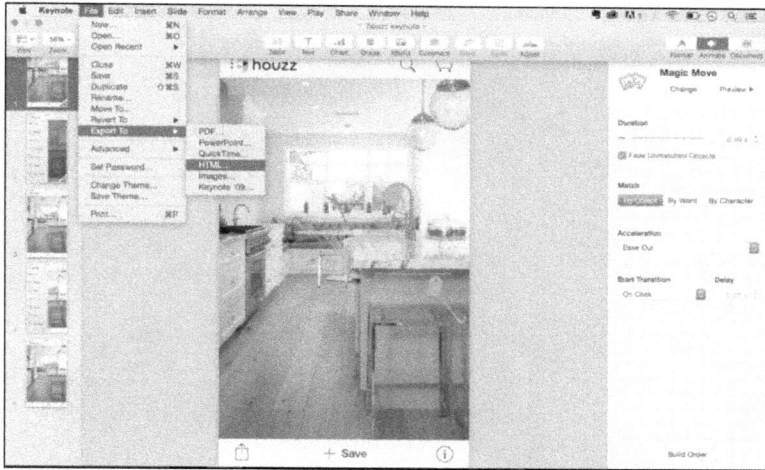

There are many times where I've built backend functionality that I wanted to confirm was configured properly. However, I realized that if the client saw an ugly user interface, they wouldn't be able to appreciate the work that was performed. So, I took a play out of the Google Venture's playbook and I created a Keynote slide deck. I designed the deck to mimic the user interface that I planned on eventually adding.

From there, I simply loaded the slides with the behavior I had built into the actual application. This approach worked quite well and the client was happy. More importantly, this option let the client focus on what I had built as opposed to requirements that were still on the to-do list.

This option also works quite well for mobile app demonstrations. Mobile apps are pretty complex for clients to demo on their phones. So, a slide-based approach makes it possible to show an app's design and behavior in a more efficient manner.

Summary

I hope that this has been a helpful freelance guide and will help you remotely demo work for clients.

33

Defining Project Success as a Freelance Developer

When it comes to freelancing, *defining project success* is a surprisingly challenging task.

A clear end

Imagine that you're competing in a marathon. When do you know it's the right time to stop running? For me, it's when I cross the finish line. It seems borderline insane to picture running a race without knowing where the finish line is, so why do so many freelancers work on projects without a clear concept of completion? If you don't establish mutually agreed upon project completion criteria with a client, you may find yourself subject to scope creep.

What is scope creep?

Scope creep in a project is when a client asks for changes in the application that exceed the original set of features. Many times, the client doesn't do this on purpose. A normal progression is for a client to see the development progress and then realize that they forgot a "key" feature.

When scope creep isn't scope creep

There are times when the right thing to do is incorporate the feature they're asking for. I can think of examples where the client hadn't listed a specific feature, but the feature was truly necessary and was required by pure common sense.

Recently, I headed up the development of an iOS project where the client didn't specify that a push notification needed to be directed to a post. After the application was completed, the client was frustrated that the system didn't have dynamic and clickable push notifications. I could have pointed to the fact that they never asked for the feature. However, in my mind the behavior was a common-sense feature, so I had it added for no extra cost to the client.

When scope creep goes badly

Scope creep is rarely that easy. You'll discover that typically clients will come up with new ideas and then try to get you to implement them for free. If you haven't established a clear definition for project success, you'll end up with an angry client who thinks that you're trying to overcharge him. Remember that in the client's mind they may not realize that they're asking for a feature outside of the original set of requirements. There are two ways for defining project success. We'll walk through both of them.

Based on requirements

First and foremost is the traditional approach, which is based on a set of requirements. This approach is OK; however, it rarely works in the real world. This process goes through the following workflow:

1. Write out a comprehensive set of project requirements.
2. The requirements sound something like: user should be able to log in.
3. Each feature has its own requirement.
4. Once all the requirements are implemented, the project is considered complete.

Theoretically, this seems like a great plan. However, in real-world projects, it rarely works. The issue is mainly that even the most experienced developer or project manager won't be able to list every... single... little feature. What will happen is that features will be missed and either you or the client is going to have to compromise to get the project completed.

Chapter 33

Based on a story

So, if defining project success based on requirements isn't practical, what's a better approach? Personally, I have had the most success by building easy-to-follow application stories. What is an application story? Let's take a look at one I wrote for a recent project:

When an admin user logs into the application she will be shown a custom dashboard that renders all the projects that she manages. From there she can edit project details. She also can navigate to the resource section, user management dashboard, and user audit log.

Notice how a story is different from a set of requirements? When clients are presented with stories it is easier for them to visualize the final product. This leads to them supplying you with the full set of required behavior in the beginning, instead of at the end. Lastly, well-constructed user stories give you a clear definition of project success. Are the stories functioning properly? Then the project is completed, it's that easy.

The sign off

After the client has approved the full set of application stories, make sure to get a formal sign off from the client. Typically, this means having them sign a document that contains all the stories. This provides a practical agreement that you can point to when all the features have been implemented.

Summary

I hope that this has been a helpful guide for defining project success as a freelancer and that you can use this approach on your next project.

34

Top Project Management Tools for Freelancers

In this chapter, I'm going to discuss the top project management tools I've used on coding projects. In preparing for this chapter, I went through some directories that listed all the known project management software applications on the market.

To be 100% honest, I was a bit shocked. There are literally thousands of project management options available to freelancers. Thankfully, I've been able to work for a number of clients and worked with various project management apps over the years.

For this chapter, I want to give you a list of the top project management tools along with their respective strengths and weaknesses. With this knowledge, you can decide on which one is the best fit for your project and freelance business.

The following are six of the top project management tools that I've used. I've probably used around a dozen tools; however, I only wanted to list applications that:

- I had actually used on production projects
- I had a good experience with and that I'd recommend to others

Top project management tools

We'll now look at each tool one by one.

Basecamp

My favorite application for project management is Basecamp. I'm probably partial to it since its founder, David Heinemeier Hansson, also happens to be the creator of the Ruby on Rails framework, which I use daily:

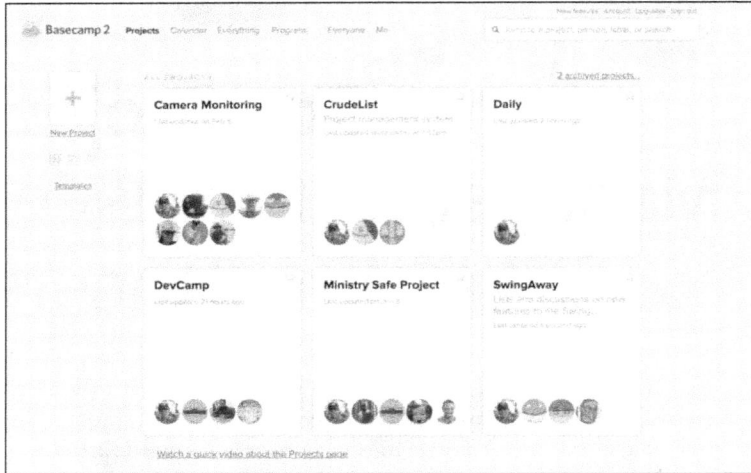

With that being said, Basecamp has a clean interface focused around to-dos and messaging. Here is a set of the to-dos assigned to me and various DevCamp team members right now:

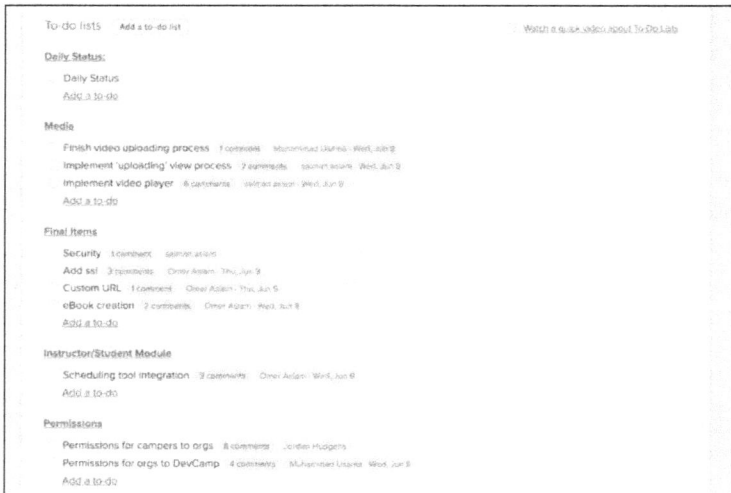

In addition to project management, I also use Basecamp as my daily planner. Essentially, I move each of my to-dos from one day to another. I like how I can have a number of my projects and their respective to-do lists all shown on one page, as shown here:

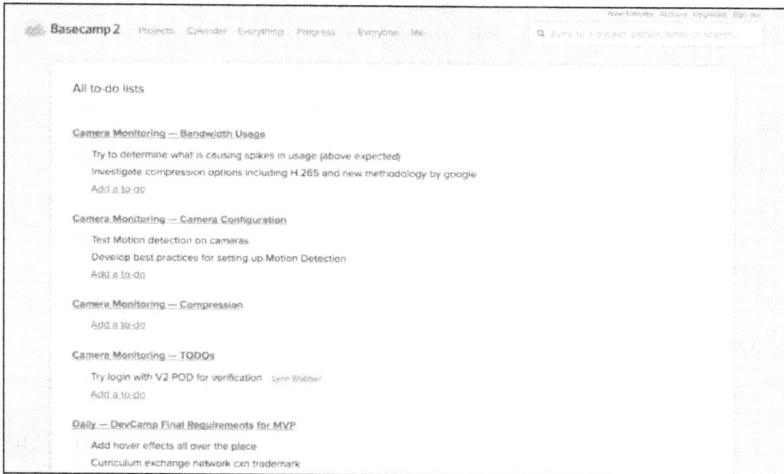

And for when I'm wanting a filtered list of what is assigned to myself, I can see only the projects that I'm tagged in as the owner:

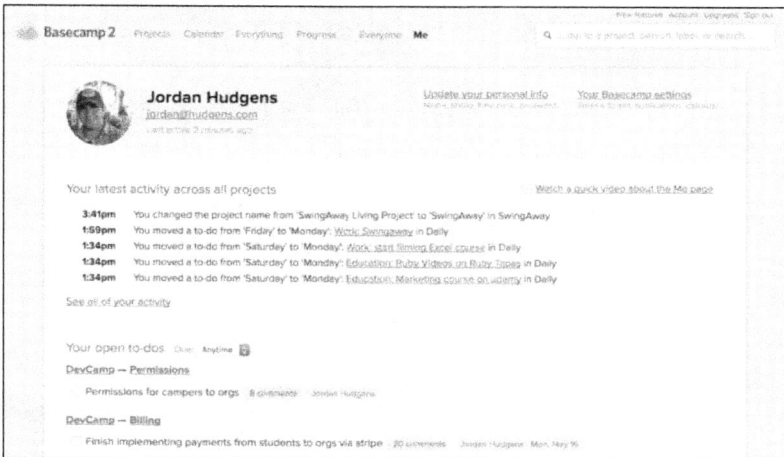

For the negatives of using Basecamp, depending on your prior experience with project management software, Basecamp may not feel very natural. If you're used to dashboards based on Gantt charts and similar tracking mechanisms, Basecamp will take some getting used to.

It does have the ability to have all those features via their add-on module. However, at its core Basecamp focuses more on messaging between team members, to-do lists, and scheduling.

Basecamp also doesn't have the best suite of mobile options, I have its iOS app on my phone. However, it's not the most intuitive, especially when compared with a few of its competitors such as Trello.

With that being said, Basecamp is still my go-to choice when it comes to project management software due to its simplicity, speed, and because I'm drawn to its to-do list structure.

Trello

Another great tool that I've used on a large number of projects is Trello. Trello utilizes a Kanban style of project management. Kanban is a workflow popularized by lean manufacturing proponents, and at a high level it uses the concept of moving cards through different stages of a project's development until they're complete:

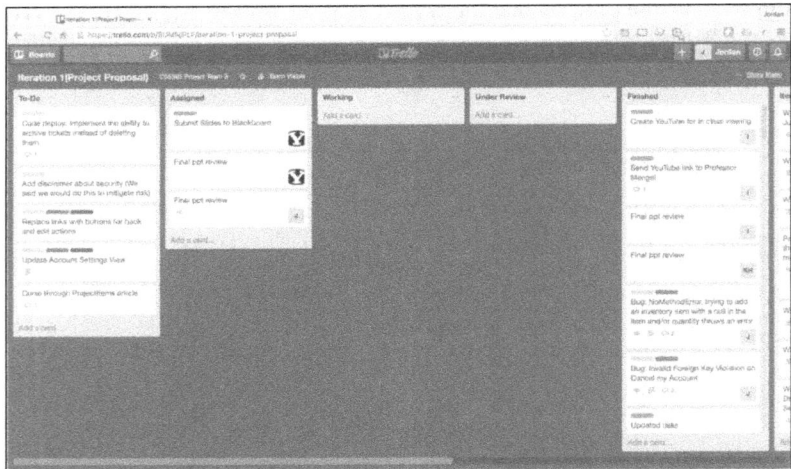

Trello essentially gives you a virtual Kanban board and lets you move tasks through each stage of the product development life cycle. For example, here in the image I would move a task from being a **To-Do** to being **Assigned**, to **Working**, to **Under Review**, and finally to **Finished**:

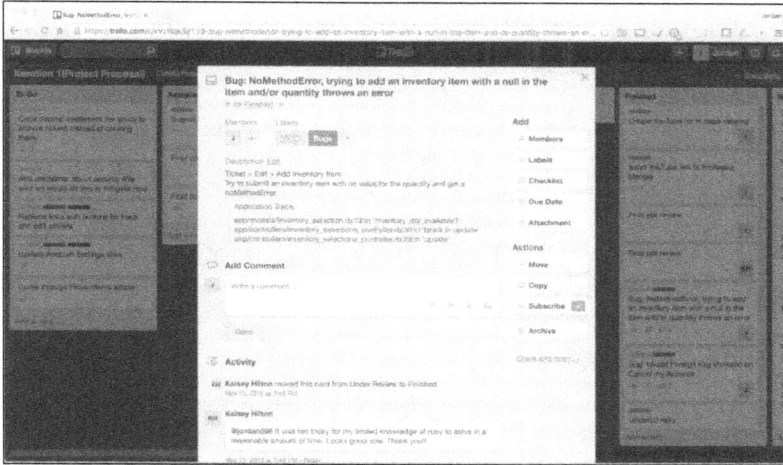

This approach makes it straightforward to visualize each task that's assigned to you, and it also has a good interface for managing a team of developers.

I also like how you can add images and attachments to tasks, which lets you encapsulate all of a task's conversations, data, and statuses in a single screen. Another bonus that Trello offers is that it works nicely on smartphones and tablets, so it's easy to track the progress of applications when you're not at your desk.

Trello has worked well for me on small-to-medium sized projects, but for large projects or complex applications I'll usually opt for Basecamp or the next one on the list: LeanKit.

LeanKit

When I was managing an entire IT organization, LeanKit was the software I went with for tracking the projects that were being worked on. It doesn't have the attractive user interface that Trello offers and it takes longer to learn.

However, it worked quite well for me when I was managing very large-scale projects, such as enterprise application rollouts to 800+ employees.

Much like Trello, LeanKit utilizes the Kanban strategy of project management. However, it focuses more on enterprises compared with smaller teams. The mobile and tablet applications offered by LeanKit were intuitive and helped me to manage projects even when I was traveling, which was a nice bonus.

LeanKit's strength is in how well it allows you to nest and organize projects and subprojects. After you've learned how the system works, it's relatively straightforward to manage large teams.

One of the biggest negatives of LeanKit was something that I considered very odd. They have a pretty archaic method for payment that requires quite a bit of manual work. I remember times where I was forced to contact the company via email simply to add new users to our account plan. This wasn't a deal killer for me. However, it does make it a poor choice for freelancers who want to work multiple projects from the same account.

ProWorkflow

ProWorkflow is one of the more standard project management options on this list of top project management tools. It does a good job of combining features such as timelines, task management, and working with teams. I only worked one project that utilized ProWorkflow. However, it was a good experience and I didn't have any complaints using the software.

Wrike

I have a bit of a love/hate relationship with Wrike as a project management tool. If you're managing a team of developers, Wrike is a great application to use. As a project manager, you're able to use it to see the status of each project along with detailed analytics for every task that is being worked on.

However, if you are a developer working on Wrike, there is a pretty steep learning curve. I would like to think that I'm pretty adept at understanding how to use a new piece of software. However, I kept getting lost in Wrike's dashboard and had a difficult time finding where to post updates to clients. Eventually, I asked the client to go through a screen sharing session where we walked through each dashboard that I would use.

With all that being said, Wrike is a good option if you're managing a team of freelancers on multiple projects, and that's why I put it on this list.

GitHub

This may seem like an odd option to put on a list of top project management tools since technically, GitHub doesn't market itself as project management software.

However, when I'm working on a project that only has developers, I've found that using GitHub's issue tracking module doubles as a project management tool:

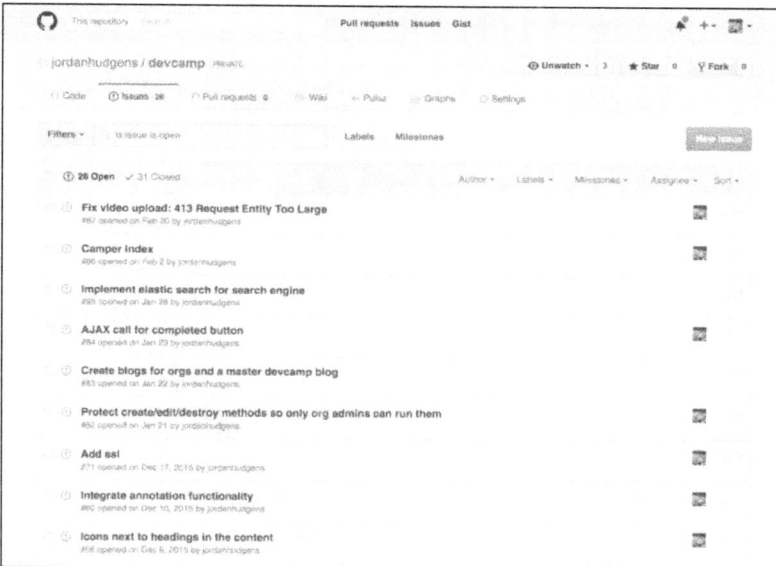

And it makes sense since some of the largest frameworks and languages are open source projects that base all the tasks on issues and features that can be easily tracked on GitHub:

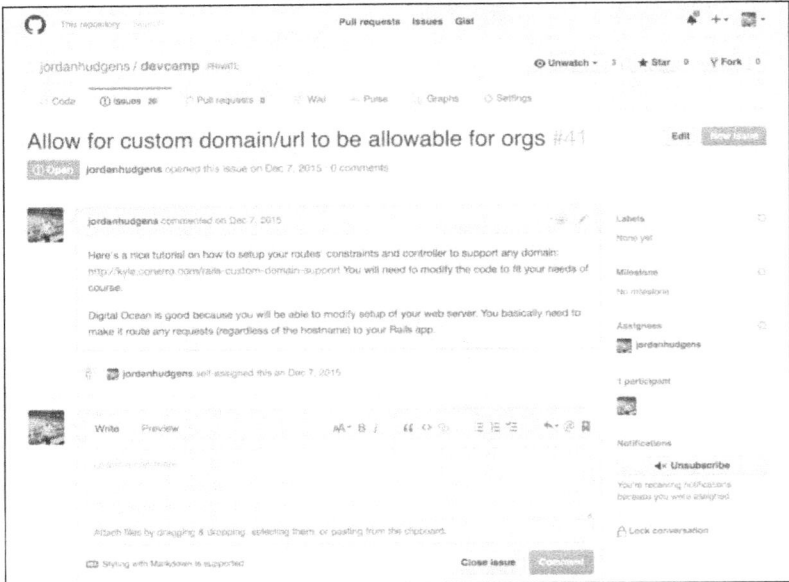

As you can see in this screenshot of a specific issue, you're able to:

- Create issues, which can also be features
- Assign users to each task
- Add links and images via the Markdown syntax
- Mark the issue as being completed

Additionally, with an experienced development team, using GitHub to manage a project has the added benefit of making task management efficient. For example, developers can close tasks automatically based on Git commits. And the easier you make a piece of software to use, the more development teams are going to like it.

Summary

I hope that this has been a helpful list of the top project management tools that you can use in your development projects and that it will help you decide on what software to use on your next project!

35

Top Freelance Bookkeeping Options for Developers

In this chapter, I'm going to review the top freelance bookkeeping options. Keeping track of finances is probably one of my least favorite parts of being a freelancer. To properly manage a freelance business, you have to manage a wide range of accounting components:

- Profit and loss reports to capture your overall profitability
- Aging reports to see how long it takes to get paid
- Expense logging to ensure you capture all potential deductions
- Accounts receivable system so that you can get paid
- Project tracking tools if you're working on large-scale projects for clients

Freelance bookkeeping options

I've used a number of bookkeeping solutions over the years, and the following are some of the ones that I've had the best experience with.

FreshBooks

FreshBooks is the system that I use for my freelance business. As far as accounting software goes, it covers 100% of the requirements I have:

Thankfully, it is also easy to use, which means that I didn't have to spend time learning how to use the software. It has an intuitive interface and allows me to log in, perform whatever tasks I have to, and then get back to working.

How it works

Here's an important screen for me in FreshBooks:

On this page, I can:

- Select a client.
- Add additional accounting information. This includes items such as a purchase order number.
- Add items to the invoice. I also like how easy it is to add fractional quantity units. If I worked a little over 14 hours, I can enter 14.1 hours and FreshBooks calculates the amount.
- Enter the payment method. This portion of the system makes it easy to let clients know if I want to be paid via standard PayPal, PayPal Business, or via FreshBooks's payment system.
- Add comments. You can post any additional information that will be sent to the client.

FreshBooks additional features

It would take hours to go through the full system, so I will simply gloss over some of the other features I find the most useful:

- **Invoice sending flexibility**: As great as it is to send invoices electronically, I still have a few clients who prefer paper-based invoices. Thankfully, not only does FreshBooks allow me to print out invoices, they actually mail them for me directly to the client.
- **Expense tracking**: Tracking business expenses is a tedious exercise. However, with the FreshBooks mobile app I can take pictures from my phone, enter the expense details, and the expense will be logged into the system.
- **Creating estimates**: In the past, I would create an estimate in Excel or Word, and then send it to the client. If they approved it I would then have to enter the details into an invoice. However, with FreshBooks I can create an estimate and email that directly to the client. If they decide to move forward with the project, the estimate will automatically transfer into an invoice.

Weaknesses

As much as I love the FreshBooks system, it does have a few weaknesses. First and foremost, it can get a little expensive if you get a large number of clients. Also, if you start hiring a large number of employees it can become a little unwieldy to manage. Personally, I'd recommend using Freshbooks for any business with under 20 employees. When you grow beyond that point, you'll want to move to a more scalable system.

QuickBooks

If you've grown out of FreshBooks, QuickBooks may be a good option for our business. QuickBooks has been the industry leader for small business accounting software as long as I've been around. Even though the company has acquired the reputation for being difficult to manage, over the past few years they've done a good job in making the system more flexible.

When you list all the potential features needed by accounting software for a small business, QuickBooks has it all. Also, due to its popularity, there is a good chance that any admins that you hire will already have experience using the system.

With all that being said, I personally wouldn't choose to use QuickBooks for DevCamp or any of the companies I work with. The main reason is because I've seen too many times where companies grow out of QuickBooks and found it very hard to migrate to a new system. I also don't like the reporting engine that the software uses. For example, if you plan on running your financial data through a big data analysis reporting engine, QuickBooks makes it difficult to export it in a format that's easy to use.

NetSuite

If your business is growing, both in clients and employees, NetSuite is a great bookkeeping option. Technically, NetSuite is probably overkill for the typical freelance business. However, if your development shop starts to turn into a full-fledged digital agency you'll need a robust ERP system. ERP systems are different from traditional bookkeeping software, they'll offer tools such as:

- **Resource planning**: This means you can allocate developer time on a project basis.
- **Advanced tax planning tools**: Once your business hits a certain size, it's important to ensure you're taking advantage of all the potential tax deductions available. Tools such as an ERP system do this for you.
- **Payroll integrations**: Being able to manage your employees, track turnover, and tasks such as that get important as your business grows. However, they're hard to track manually. A system such as NetSuite calculates all your employee tracking metrics so you can use them to manage your team.

Summary

I hope that this has been a helpful set of freelance bookkeeping options that will help you decide on the right system for your business.

36
Learning the Secret to Get New Clients as a Freelancer

If you're wanting to start a freelance business, the most pressing challenges typically revolve around getting new clients. When I initially launched my freelance business, I struggled to acquire customers.

However, after a few months of trudging through the traditional channels I discovered a great solution that resulted in generating over $290,000 in revenue last year. And it's what I want to discuss in this chapter.

Where to find new clients

Let's begin by reviewing the list of options for where you can find new clients as a freelancer. I've read countless blog posts and a number of books on the subject, and the following were the most popular recommendations:

- **Friends and family**: This may seem like a natural place to start; however it's been my experience that friends and family typically expect you to work for free or incredibly cheap. This channel can be good if you're just starting out and you need to build a portfolio; however, it is not scalable and usually not too profitable.
- **Network events**: For networking, you can join your local chamber of commerce or find networking groups where you can promote your business. This approach can work well in some cases. However, each time I've tried it I've discovered that there were already several other developers attending working on getting new clients for their own freelance businesses.

I wouldn't let my experience with this option stop you from trying it, but make sure you're prepared to compete with others. I remember attending a chamber of commerce "meet and greet" a few years ago. When everyone around the room introduced themselves and their business, there were half a dozen freelance developers who were all offering the same services.

- Outsourcing services. This is the option that I want to focus on here. Interestingly enough, I was told by a number of freelance "experts" that this avenue was too difficult. However, I found a great way to use it for getting new clients as a freelancer.

The challenge in getting new clients with outsourcing services

As I have already mentioned, I had a difficult time in the beginning getting new clients. Using services such as oDesk and Elance (which have now merged and are now Upwork) were especially challenging. Even though I had a solid portfolio and a decade of experience, I couldn't get a single client. Some of the challenges were the following:

1. I didn't have any ratings or reviews. Not many clients are willing to take a risk on a developer without some type of recommendation from others.

2. I was priced higher than the majority of other freelancers. The majority of the freelance teams marketing services on outsourcing sites are offshore. This meant that I was having to compete against developers offering to work for, at times, 90% cheaper than my rate. I charge $100 per hour, while the majority of offshore teams are charging $10-$20 per hour.

3. I didn't have the time to pitch each potential client. In regard to marketing my freelance services, I was very streaky. I would get motivated for a few days and send out a large number of pitches. And then I would get depressed that I wasn't getting any replies and I wouldn't send any proposals for weeks.

After struggling for a few months, I knew I didn't have any control over challenges #1 or #2. However, I could do something about #3. I was working a full-time job at the time, while also attending grad school, so my time was very limited. With that in mind I came up with a marketing system. And it actually worked!

Chapter 36

Getting new clients as a freelancer

Since I'm a little bit on the stubborn side it took me a while to admit it, but I finally came to terms with the fact that I wasn't getting new clients as a freelancer, especially with the methods that I'd been trying up to that time. So, I put a plan into action that involved hiring some freelancers of my own. I assembled a team that helped fill in my weak areas.

To start getting new clients as a freelancer, I knew I had to have clearly written proposals that described my services. And I also knew that the proposals would have to be sent out 24/7.

Proposal material

With that in mind I researched sales copy writers on Upwork and hired a talented marketer who created three different proposals that I could use.

This included sales copy that advertised my experience, portfolio, and expertise as a developer. I had three versions created because I wanted each one to be targeted to a specific type of project. For example, one of the proposals focused on enterprise projects. Another proposal was targeted at building APIs, while the third had content geared toward startups.

Sending out constant proposals

With a full set of professional proposals, I was ready to implement the second step of my plan: consistently sending out proposals. For this, I hired a detail-oriented and fluent virtual assistant from the Philippines named Sy.

I could hire Sy for $6.50 an hour and he paid for himself in the first week! I walked him through the proposals and described the types of projects that I wanted to get hired for.

After I was confident that Sy clearly understood my goals, I let him loose on Elance. He reviewed the full set of potential projects on the marketplace and sent my targeted proposals to each project that fit my criteria. Within a week I was getting responses back from clients and within two weeks I had been hired for multiple projects. Three months later, I had to hire my own developers because I was getting so many clients hiring me to build applications.

The result

So how did my strategy for getting new clients as a freelancer work out? Well, here is a screenshot of my FreshBooks dashboard. Last year, my freelance business generated over $290,000 in revenue:

One month hit over $40,000:

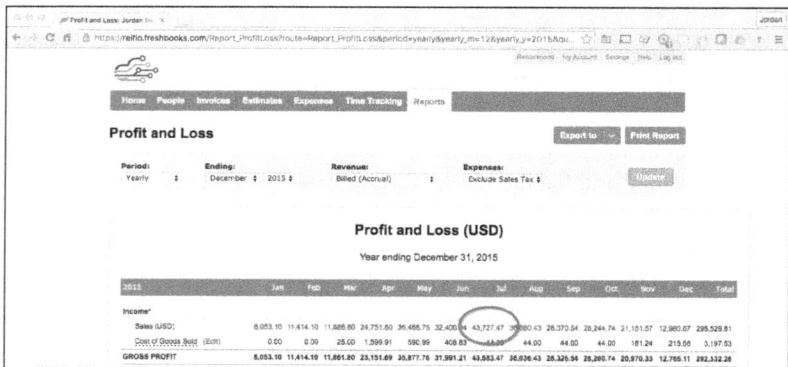

I'm not going to pretend that this was easy. This is pretty much the opposite of a get-rich-quick kind of scheme. However, by implementing this strategy, I could cost-efficiently outsource the marketing for my freelance business so that I could focus on actual development.

Summary

I hope that this has been a helpful guide for getting new clients as a freelancer and has given you some ideas on how you can build your own business.

37

Managing Client Conflicts as a Freelancer

In this chapter, I'm going to discuss *managing client conflicts*. It's simply a matter of life and business that you will run into conflicts with clients. Some of the most common confrontations seem to be:

- Going over the time you originally estimated
- Going over the budget for the project
- Not delivering a feature that matched the client's expectations
- A bug occurring in an application

None of these are fun to work through, and most of them can be avoided if the proper care is taken at each stage of the project management process. However, I want to discuss what happens when conflicts occur and how to best manage them.

Strategies for managing client conflicts

First and foremost, do not let emotions take over. This is probably one of the hardest ones for me because I love what I do and when bad things happen in a project my first response is to get defensive, which is one of the worst responses to have. So, when I see an angry message come through from a client or take a phone call, I make sure that before I respond I sit back and try to look at the situation from the client's perspective.

It's pretty rare that a client will get upset for no reason. The majority of people are rational and prefer to stay away from confrontation, so if the client is mad there is probably a legitimate reason for it. Therefore, the first step I take is pretending that I'm the client and then I feel like I can give a better response from that perspective.

If a project went over budget and I'm imagining that I'm the client, I can understand why they're not happy because I don't like spending more money on something than I originally was told it would cost. So instead of responding with some defensive messages, such as:

"It wasn't my fault, you were the ones that changed the scope"

Or

"I can't control that the fact that the designer took twice as long to deliver the mocks"

I'll start with saying things that show that I understand their perspective, for example I'll say:

"I completely understand how frustrating it is, the project scope has grown and it's been hard to meet all of the requirements based on the original timeline"

Or

"I am sorry, I should have allotted more time for the design phase, it's my fault and I will work to get it taken care of"

If you pretend that you're a client hearing those four responses, which ones would put you more at ease? The ones where I was defensive and tried to blame everyone else or the ones where I took responsibility for the project and gave a calm reply?

The easy thing to do in a confrontation is to become defensive or respond aggressively; however, neither of those approaches will fix the issue and they'll most likely make things worse.

Your first goal when a conflict arises between yourself and a client should be to see if you can see the issue from their perspective.

With that being said, there will be times where the core problem is the client's fault. They may be very bad at stating project requirements or they may simply be poor communicators. I once had a client who hired me a few years ago and asked me to build an application and simply gave me about 4-5 screenshots from another website and then they completely disappeared. I did my best to build what I guessed they wanted and I sent daily updates to them, and then a month later he messaged me furious that the app wasn't what he wanted and then went on to list all of the features it was missing, even though they were features he had never asked for originally.

Chapter 37

I calmly fired him as a client on the spot and informed him that I wouldn't be able to work on the project any longer. I didn't raise my voice, I didn't explain how he gave me little to no guidance for building the app, but I knew it wasn't the type of client I could work effectively for.

I hope that this has been a good set of tips for how to manage conflict with your clients. I did quite a bit of research on this guide prior to writing it to see if there were any things that I was missing and I discovered a full library could be made out of the information based on conflict resolution.

There are discussions about personality types and more acronyms than I care to list here, however, what I've written for you in this guide is what I've used over the years and it's worked very well for me through a number of challenging situations and many different client personality types. I'm confident it will also work well for you and your clients.

38

Examples of Freelance Portfolios That Help Acquire New Clients

In this chapter, I'm going to discuss *examples of freelance portfolios* that you can use to attract clients. Before deciding on the types of projects you want to include in your portfolio, it's important to answer a few key questions:

- Who will I be showing this portfolio to?
- What type of features do I love developing?

The first question is pretty standard; you need to know you your audience to ensure that your work will have its greatest impact. For example, if you want to attract small mom and pop businesses, it wouldn't make much sense to fill your portfolio with 3D Unity zombie game renderings.

The second question speaks to your passions as a developer. Too many coders create a portfolio full of generic projects that they don't truly love and it's apparent to potential employers and clients. Make sure that the projects you build fit your personality as a developer and that you are happy with the end result. Portfolio projects are not an item meant to be simply crossed off your developer checklist, they should be projects that you're personally proud of and enjoyed building.

Examples of freelance portfolios

The following examples of freelance portfolio projects entail a comprehensive feature set and should impress a wide variety of clients. However, they are simply starting points, not hard and fast rules.

Social network utility

This is where you build a basic social network with a clean design and features such as having posts, followers, and comments, and integrate at least one unique/advanced feature, such as giving users the ability to edit each other's posts.

When I'm looking to hire a new developer, I like to see that they know how to work comfortably with complex data models such as the ones required by a social networking application, and being able to work with advanced permissions structures is very important, so this makes a good portfolio project.

An API tool

An example would be to develop a search engine for Stack Overflow that enables more advanced features than the main web application. A project like this would show that you can work with APIs and can implement a search engine feature.

An accounting application

You don't have to rebuild QuickBooks. However, an accounting project can illustrate that you know how to work with financial calculations, callbacks, advanced database queries, and information security.

A scheduling application

I've built several scheduling applications. This type of app will show that you know how to work with dates and times (which is no easy task for any developer), along with complex validations.

A frontend application

Create an app using a frontend framework such as AngularJS or React and integrate it with a server-side backend such as Ruby on Rails. This will show that you know how to work with service-based architecture and design, which is a prerequisite for my clients.

Chapter 38

If you build these apps (or apps that contain the same level of sophistication), you will be able to clearly showcase your expertise to potential clients, colleagues, and future employers. These projects will also give you a great code library that you can reference for future projects.

I've lost count of how many times I've reviewed past portfolio projects to see how I implemented a specific feature so I could use it on an app I was working on at the moment. I hope this list has inspired you to build out your own portfolio of projects.

39

Importance of Test-Driven Development for Coders

Let's discuss the importance of **test-driven development**. First and foremost, if the terms TDD or BDD, which are short for test- and behavior-driven development, are foreign to you, they are the practice of building code tests for applications.

And even more specifically, TDD and BDD are *software development processes in which you create a test that sets an expectation before implementing any code.*

An example of using TDD to create a feature for returning a full name from a user class would be to:

1. Create a test that calls a new method, such as full_name, that combines the first and last name of a user and returns a string combining the names into a single value:

```
Create a Test for the feature

full_name(first, last)
#=→ "Jordan Hudgens"
```

2. Then we'd run the test, knowing that it will fail:

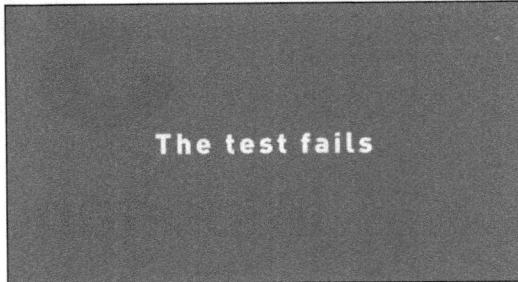

The test fails

3. Then we would go and add a barebones implementation of the code:

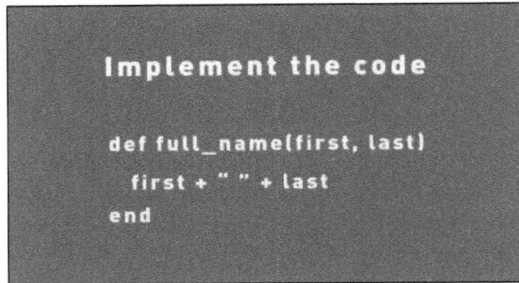

Implement the code

```
def full_name(first, last)
    first + " " + last
end
```

This will get the test passing:

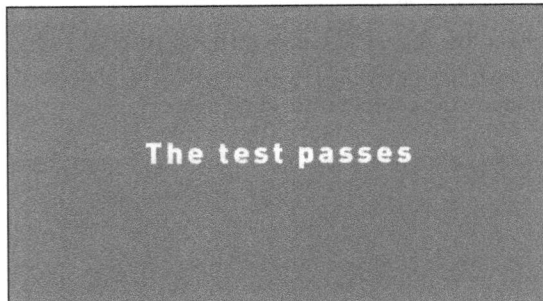

The test passes

4. Then we'd go back and refactor the implementation to ensure it conforms to best practices and that the refactor doesn't break anything:

This process is known as the **Red, Green, Refactor** workflow and is a pretty standard practice across all languages and frameworks.

Importance of test-driven development

With that dead simple explanation of how TDD works, let's discuss the importance of TDD and the best way to answer this coding interview question.

There's quite a bit of debate on the topic, with a number of prominent developers who are against the practice of TDD, with one of the main arguments being that many coders don't use it properly and are essentially just testing pre-existing functionality instead of behavior unique to the application.

However, with that being said, if you're looking to get hired as a developer there is a very good chance that you will need to be fully versed in how to work with TDD and BDD since I don't know of very many software organizations that don't require tests.

There are four main reasons why I use TDD for all the production applications that I build or manage:

1. **Regression**: If you add a new feature into your application, you need to have 100% certainty that the new code you added won't break any pre-existing functionality in the app.

    For example, if I create a new method that will break if any nil values are passed to it and I call that method on legacy data that could contain some nil values, I want to know that before the new feature goes live. Without tests, I'd have to go and manually test every part of the application each time I implement a new piece of functionality. However, if I have a full test suite I can simply run the tests, and if they're all passing it is a good indicator that the new changes can be pushed live.

2. **Team management**: If you're managing a team, having a team of developers that follows TDD processes will give you a level of transparency into what they're doing. In fact, in Kent Beck's book *Extreme Programming*, Beck says that testing is one of the biggest keys for a development process to stay on track and budget.

3. **Documentation**: When an application that was built with TDD is finished, the tests should be able to provide 100% of the documentation for the software. Certain testing frameworks, such as RSpec, even have the ability to print out tests in a documentation form that provides a full description on the app's behavior and can be understood even by non-technical individuals.

4. **Leads the development process**: One of the most important keys to writing good software is to break code into as many small, manageable chunks as possible. When you use TDD you should naturally write small methods, efficient class definitions, and you should have minimal code bloat. When you're following TDD practices the tests themselves should lead the software's development, and the end result should be a well-organized and scalable code base.

One caveat to TDD is that testing is pointless if the test suite is not well structured. If you simply create a myriad of tests that do nothing more than test the core functionality of a language or framework, your test suite isn't going to have any benefit. However, if you build an application and let the tests drive your development and code structure, you will end up with a great application that you should be proud of.

For further information, I recommend reading the full series by *Martin Fowler*, which is seen as one of the most in-depth discussions on TDD ever produced.

Summary

I hope that this chapter will help you answer questions relating to the importance of TDD, and good luck with the interview!

40

SEO Best Practices and Strategies for Freelancers

If you build applications that users access on the web, you have most likely been asked by clients to provide an SEO-friendly website to help drive new customers to their site. You may also have realized that the world of SEO is so expansive that you could spend the rest of your career studying it and you still wouldn't have it mastered.

With that being said, I've found that if I follow a set of SEO best practices, the websites I create are search engine-friendly and clients are happy with the organic traffic sent their way. Search trends seem to change on a daily basis, and I personally don't have time to keep track of each Google search algorithm change. Instead, I focus on SEO best practices and they have worked well for me and they follow search engine white hat marketing practices so that I don't risk getting penalized by Google or Bing.

SEO best practices tutorial

First and foremost, *content is king*. Unique quality content is always going to be the most important criteria for SEO.

Content is king

Coming from someone who has spent countless hours studying Google's search algorithm from a computer science perspective, I can say that all the algorithm is attempting to do is connect search users with the best, most relevant content that they're looking for.

All the nuances to the algorithm, such as page ranking, counting links, and so on, are all simply ways that Google is trying to automatically find the best content on the internet. With that being said, quality content by itself is not a guarantee of traffic, but without it you won't be able to gain search engine traction for very long.

One question I get asked quite often is how many words a post should be. My answer is always "*let the content determine the wordcount.*" A good rule of thumb is to have around 500-1,500 words per post, but don't waste time worrying about hitting a specific word count, focus on creating high-quality content and the word count will take care of itself.

Creating an XML sitemap

Next, make sure that your site has a XML sitemap that you supply to Google and Bing. This will make it much easier for the search engines to index your pages. The best content in the world won't be found on a search engine if Google's spider can't find it.

Mixing text, images, and videos

Third, users, and therefore search engines, like seeing images and video on pages. A very important criteria for following SEO best practices is to have a solid mix of text, images, and videos on a page. This helps not only for standard searches, but also for Google Image search, which can be another great source of website traffic.

Managing your site speed

Fourth, there is site speed. Kissmetrics research shows that sites with slow load times have dramatically higher page abandonment rates, and not only is this bad for business, but your ranking with Google will decrease if your site is slow.

Site responsiveness

Fifth is the important modern SEO best practice of site responsiveness. Responsiveness is the ability of your site to dynamically adjust in size and layout based on the device viewing it. This is about making you're your site looks and works great on, say, a standard web browser, a tablet, and a smartphone. Search engines have added responsiveness as a key criteria for site rankings, since traffic coming from mobile users is now so significant.

Chapter 40

Backlinks

Sixth are the backlinks to your site. Now this is a dangerous one, because backlinks used to be the top criteria that determined a site's page rank. I remember around 15 years ago when I started building websites that if I could get a popular site to link to a site I published, the new site would start getting search engine traffic and would show up higher in search results within 24 hours.

However, quite a bit has changed and now backlinks aren't as important as they used to be, but they are still very helpful. I mentioned that backlinks could be dangerous because Google has gotten ridiculously good at detecting users trying to game the system. If you use black hat techniques for acquiring backlinks you'll soon find your site penalized or even completely delisted from Google entirely.

So, what I do now for backlinks is to message journalists and other bloggers using tools such as HARO and contribute quotes and perform interviews on other sites. In return, they will typically link to one of my sites.

This is a slower way of building backlinks, but in the long run it's a good strategy. Google also watches for sites that offer to charge you to guest post and link back to your site, so I'd strongly recommend to stay away from those types of service.

Focused content

The last for this list is for your content to be focused. If you are shooting an arrow, it helps to have a target and when you're writing a blog post or publishing a page, it's important to have a keyword to target. When I'm creating content, I select a phrase and aim to have the entire content revolve around it.

Without a focus word or phrase, it will be difficult for your post to gain traction. So, make sure you always stay focused with each post that you create. There are also plenty of great tools out there for ensuring that you're following search engine best practices. Generally, I use a tool called Yoast that uses a checkbox approach to each post.

Summary

I hope that this has been a helpful summary of SEO best practices that you can utilize in your own projects and help you drive more traffic to you or your clients' site.

41

Client Communication Freelancing Tips

When I was originally building up my freelance business, I heard a common complaint from clients talking about previous developers that worked on their projects: poor communication and a lack of transparency.

As a developer, I know how easy it is to fall into the trap of wanting to dive into the code and build a project. However, without proper client communication you'll run into the following issues:

- Clients will think that no work is being performed. Regardless of reality, if you don't tell a client what you did their first assumption is going to be that you didn't do anything. This can get very messy when you send your bill and the hours that you charged don't match what the client estimated based on your updates.

- You may be building a feature in a way that the client didn't expect. I've had it happen a number of times where I understood a requirement to mean one thing, but the client had a completely different expectation in mind.

While the immediate reaction to try and fix communication issues may be to be in constant communication with the client, this approach will waste your time and it will also give them the mindset that you'll always be available, which will limit your freedom, which kills one of the main reasons you became a freelancer in the first place.

A system to maintain proper client communication

With these issues in mind, if you can perfect this part of being a freelancer, you'll see that it leads to happy customers while also being a healthy environment for you as a freelancer.

I've put together a system for client communication that is balanced, meaning that the client will feel informed about the project but it will not inhibit your personal freedom:

1. Create a project management dashboard. I'll typically use Basecamp or Trello; however, you can use anything that you prefer and is easy for the client to use.

2. At the beginning of the day, schedule when you'll work on the project. Each morning I write down on a dry erase board all the projects I'm going to work on, and I list what time slots I'm going to work on them. For example, I'm going to work on a Rails project for XYZ client from 2 PM to 3.30 PM.

3. After the schedule is set, I message the clients and I let them know when I'll be working on their project, so they can contact me during that time slot if they need something immediate. In this way. they will also know that work is going to be performed that day.

4. After each project time slot that day, I post on the project dashboard an update on the tasks that were worked on that day. Because I like being efficient with time, I'll usually copy and paste the GitHub commit comments as bullet points.

Summary

If you follow this system, your clients will be happy because they will know what you're doing each day, and it lets you stay in control of your schedule.

42

Outsource Web Developers Properly with System-Based Processes

When it comes to working on client projects, I've worked on applications ranging from apps that I could build in a few days to applications that have taken over a year of development time and involved over a dozen different developers. So, what the best way to work with outsource web developers?

Whenever I have a large project that requires a development team that I need to bring onboard, it presents a series of challenges, such as:

- Do the programmers specialize in the features that need to be built out?
- Will bringing on other developers allow the project to stay on budget?
- How can I make sure that the code quality meets the client expectations?

I could pretend that the outsource web developers I've worked with were managed properly for every project, but that would be not be telling you the truth. In fact, I decided to write this chapter based on the many times that I've had poor experiences managing development teams.

A system to manage outsourced web developers

Based on my mixed experiences in managing outsourced web developers, I've built the following system to ensure that I have picked the right set of developers and that they are producing code that will help make clients happy:

1. **Automated testing**: Whether you work by yourself or with outsourced developers, it's vital that you use automated testing. This can include BDD or unit testing. However, this process will help to ensure that all the features of an application are working and also that new features do not break pre-existing functionality.

2. **Daily reports**: Depending on the situation that you have with your clients, it's important that you receive daily reports on the development work performed for that day. If you're not getting daily updates there is a good chance that no work was performed.

3. **Access to applications**: If you happen to only be managing the application and not actually developing, make sure that you have proper access. This includes command-line database access, your public keys on the server that the application is being deployed on, and any error logging system, such as Honeybadger or AppSignal.

Summary

If you're bringing on an outsourced development team, it typically means that your time is limited. However, if you follow these three steps, it should help your project to be successful.

43

How to Create Accurate Freelance Bids?

Being able to give good estimates is one of the most critical tasks you can do as a freelancer. If you quote too low, you'll end up with an angry customer because even if you did great work, he's having to pay more than he budgeted. And if you bid too high, there's a good chance you won't get the job and the potential client will go to a competitor who gave a lower bid.

Over the years, I've been guilty of erring on both sides of the spectrum and I've had to deal with the consequences. Those consequences were not fun, which is why I've put together a formula for you in this chapter that I follow for building bids:

1. Get a detailed drill down of the project requirements. Without this you won't be able to create an accurate bid no matter what else you do. Imagine if an architect had to give an estimate to a client who said, "I want a nice house with a cool fence." He wouldn't be able to accurately estimate how much the house would cost to build. An architect will get a detailed breakdown of square footage, number of bedrooms, along with a list of all the bells and whistles. In the same way, you need a detailed breakdown of every feature that the application needs to have.

2. After you have the list of features, break them into categories, such as: database setup, frontend design, user permission configurations, and so on. And then put each of the features into one of the category buckets.

3. Put all the data into a spreadsheet segmented by the categories you created in step two.

4. Give a conservative estimate on each feature in the spreadsheet.

5. Have the spreadsheet tally up the total hours or cost and that is the project estimate.

Does this formula seem like common sense? Good, because *creating accurate freelance bids* should be a simple process!

If you came up and asked me how long it would take to build a payroll system, I wouldn't have a clue what the bid should be. However, I do know how long building a user database will take, and I know how long it will take to implement the design, and so on. And by breaking down the project into small, specific chunks, I'm now able to feel more confident about how long the individual features will take to build.

I also update the spreadsheet as I progress through the project. That way, I'll actually have a guide for future projects. For example, if I originally estimated that building a video upload feature would take 8 hours but it ended up taking 14 hours, I will be able to more accurately estimate that feature in future projects.

Summary

I hope that this has been a helpful chapter for learning how to systematize your process for creating estimates as a freelancer.

44

Freelancer Tips – Three Ways to Get New Clients

In this chapter, I'm going to discuss some strategies that I've used successfully over the years for getting new clients. There have been three main ways that I've gotten new clients:

- Outsourcing services such as oDesk and Elance (which have now merged to be Upwork)
- LinkedIn
- Referrals

So, I'll now share some of the ways that I've had success in each one of those channels so that you can take on some of the experiences I've had and apply them to your own freelance career.

Freelancing services

Freelance services such as Upwork are great for finding new clients. The keys to success are to constantly send out proposals, dozens per day, and be quick to communicate with potential clients.

If you're a US- or UK-based developer, make sure you understand that you'll be competing from developers from all over the world, which means that the bids that you'll be competing with could be dramatically lower than what you'd want to charge. However, I've been able to get dozens of long-term clients from these services, including large organizations such as Eventbrite and Quip.

LinkedIn

LinkedIn is an interesting tool for freelancers. I've gotten several clients from the service simply by having a filled-out profile and joining user groups for the languages and frameworks that I specialize in.

I've gotten clients such as AppDev and the Flatiron School from LinkedIn. Interestingly enough, I was never proactive with reaching out to clients. If you have a good profile showcasing your skills and you have joined enough groups, jobs start to come in. It's incremental growth, but I've found some great clients though LinkedIn.

Referrals

Referrals are one of the best ways to get clients. This marketing channel typically takes the most time depending on your own social and client network. When I say referral, I'm not simply referencing referrals from other clients, I've gotten referrals from coworkers, friends, family, and through networking events, such as local Chamber of Commerce organizations.

Summary

I hope this has been a helpful chapter to different freelancer strategies to grow your client base. If you're an employer who works with freelancers, then I hope you also read this section closely, and it gives you a better insight into freelancers' minds, and how to get the most from them.

Part 3

Career Skills

45

Should I Learn to Code? – A Balanced Perspective on Programming

To start off this part of the book that covers all about what it takes to have a successful career as a developer, I'm going to talk about the question: should I learn to code?

This question was sparked by the controversial post on TechCrunch by Basel Farag (https://techcrunch.com/2016/05/10/please-dont-learn-to-code/), where he urges people to not learn coding. As the founder of Rails bootcamp you may think that my reaction would be to spout off a full list of all the reasons why everyone should learn how to code, because that's good for business, right?

However, I went through his post in detail and I also reviewed a slew of response posts that called for Basel's head, denouncing him as a modern-day heretic.

Should I learn to code? – a balanced look at both sides

After going through all the content around Basel Farag's argument, my belief is that both sides of the argument have valid points that should be considered by anyone deciding whether to learn to code or not!

Let's first explore the idea that *not everyone* should learn to program. Farag proposes that coding is hard, which it is, and therefore, the dream that you can take a few online tutorials and become a professional developer is a lie… and he's 100% right about that. Development, especially for true production applications, is very hard and takes years of study to become truly proficient. It's not enough to simply learn how to build an application that lets users create records in a database from a form, for example. A professional developer needs to have expertise in:

- Managing dependencies between code libraries
- Working with object-oriented programming best practices
- Having clean code
- Implementing automated testing for continuous development
- Knowing how to transition seamlessly between various frameworks

And the list goes on and on…

In fact, even though I'm a professional developer and have worked for clients as big as Eventbrite and Chevron, I spend several hours a day going through development books and online guides to simply keep up with all of the new coding techniques and systems that are continually emerging.

So, all that is to say that Basel Farag is right in that if you want to become a professional developer, you have a challenging road ahead of you. Of course, if you make it through, you will have gained a tremendous skill and you could well find yourself in demand by a number of industries.

Let's now explore the opposite side of the argument, that everyone should learn how to code. I really appreciate the VentureBeat article by Edward Chiu (`https://venturebeat.com/2016/05/22/how-coding-kick-started-my-sales-career/`), where he describes how he went through a coding bootcamp and he did not become a professional developer… but that he did get a great job as a sales engineer that he never would have gotten if he wouldn't have learned coding!

Chapter 45

This is the side of the argument that is ignored all too often, because learning to code does not mean that you have to become a professional developer, but it will give you a new skill set that can be used across many different jobs. Steve Jobs said it best when he said:

> *"I think everybody in this country should learn how to program a computer because it teaches you how to think."*

To me, Jobs hit the nail on the head here: learning how to code is not simply a prerequisite for becoming a professional developer, even though that can happen as well. It gives your mind a system for structured thinking that you can apply across all disciplines.

From a personal example, I used to have a hard time taking notes. I would randomly write down words all over a page without any really coherent flow and when I'd look back at them later they would be completely worthless to study from. However, after I learned to code I started actually taking my notes in code form to give them structure, I'd set up loops for repeating items, classes to hold a topic's attributes and processes, and return statements for the end results of whatever I was trying to learn. That may sound nerdy, and it probably is, but it gave me an organized system for taking notes and learning new topics.

Summary

In summary, I hope that this balanced view has help you answer the question: should I learn to code?

46
Following Your Passion – Good or Bad Advice for Developers?

As a developer, should you follow your passion? I hear this term and this advice quite often and I'm not a fan of taking things at face value, so I wanted to look into the concept and review it here.

At a high level, the advice centers around the idea that if you do work in a field that you truly love, you will be happy. Many people point to Steve Job's Stanford commencement speech when he says:

> *"And most important, have the courage to follow your heart and intuition. They somehow already know what you truly want to become."*

Following your passion – a case study

While writing and researching this book, I came across Cal Newport's book, *So Good They Can't Ignore You*, where he took a deep look at Steve Job's life. He shows that if Jobs would have spent his life adhering to the advice of following your passion, he never would have started Apple, but instead would have become a Buddhist monk living in Asia.

Jobs started Apple for the practical reason that he saw a way to make some quick money selling a set of computers to a local electronics store, and that sale sparked his interest in technology. So, it seems like following your passions is not a cut and dried process of doing work that you love.

However, my advice to you is not to ignore your passions, but instead to use them to build a career that you truly love and can excel in.

Sticking with the Steve Jobs example, one of the other passions Jobs had was calligraphy, which is essentially fancy handwriting if you've never seen it before. When creating the user interface for Apple's operating system, Jobs leveraged his extensive expertise in calligraphy to integrate fonts into the programs. Here was an example of Jobs combining his passions with a practical implementation.

As developers, we're in a unique position where we can work in a wide assortment of industries: if you love sports you can work for a professional sports team, or if entertainment is your flavor then you can work for a media company. The possibilities are really endless.

One of my biggest passions is baseball. I grew up around the game and I love everything about it. I wasn't skilled enough to play professionally, but right now I'm working towards my PhD in computer science and my topic of research is big data analysis in baseball.

It wouldn't have been practical for me to waste who knows how many years trying to make it as a professional baseball player, but I can leverage my skill as a developer and still perform work that I love to do. I've also have the privilege of having multiple clients that are in the sports industry, which has allowed me to work in the sector that I'm passionate about while still leveraging the skills I have as a developer.

Summary

Hopefully, my research and personal experiences can help you decide if following your passion is the right decision, or if there is a middle group that would lead to a better end result.

47

How to Learn to Code from Scratch? – A Practical Strategy

Becoming a developer is a rewarding yet challenging task. One of the greatest blocks for people to understand programming is simply having a plan and deciding where to start.

In this chapter, I'm doing to walk through strategies to help you learn how to code from scratch. I've been a developer for a number of years. I taught myself how to code and I've witnessed a wide variety of educational techniques for learning programming over the past decade.

Some of the strategies I've seen are good, others are a waste of time. This chapter contains the strategies that have stood the test of time and will help you launch your coding journey.

Small bites

First and foremost on the list of tips to learn how to code from scratch is the principle of **small bites**.

I have a friend who trains professional and Olympic athletes for Adidas, named Mark Verstegen. Back when I used to train at his institute, he would always say something that really stuck with me. When any athlete presented a tough goal, such as qualifying for the Olympics or making it to the big leagues, he'd ask them:

"How would you eat an elephant?"

After the athlete would look at him with a confused look, he'd follow by saying:

> *"It's not a trick question, the only way to eat an elephant is one bite at a time."*

This is great advice for many aspects of life. However, I've discovered that it's an especially important concept for developers to understand. When I think back to when I was learning development, my greatest obstacles and challenges came when I tried to do too much.

For example, when I was trying to build a new feature I would attempt to code the entire feature at once. Most of the time this would end up with the program not working, and then I'd have to go through every line of code until I figured out what was wrong.

However, the more experienced I've become as a developer the more I realize the importance of breaking concepts down into small, easy-to-manage chunks.

Let's imagine that you are building a connection to the Twitter API. Instead of trying to build the entire feature, focus first on connecting to the API. Then print the values returned from Twitter. Finally, you can format the data so that it looks nice. By breaking what you're learning into small components, you'll discover that you will have a better understanding of the processes going on. You will also be able to remember how to implement the features later in real-world projects because the concepts will be more tangible.

Tutorials

Over the past few years the online educational space has grown exponentially. Whether you are looking to learn Java or Ruby, you'll be able to find countless tutorials that will help you understand programming. These types of tools most likely won't turn you into a professional developer by themselves, since achieving a professional level of skill takes years and typically requires you to work on a wide range of real-world projects.

However, tutorials can be a great introduction to programming. In addition to giving step-by-step guides for how to build applications, screencasts are also great for showing you what types of apps a specific language or framework can build. When I'm learning a new language I'll watch a full series of tutorials without even trying to type in the code. I do this so that I can familiarize myself with the capabilities of the language.

Chapter 47

One of the weaknesses with tutorials is that it's hard for them to replicate your own environment. For example, if you're working on a Java programming language tutorial from a few years ago, there's a good chance that the instructor will have a different language version than you do. This will cause some confusing bugs, and without any assistance many individuals have quit their programming dreams out of frustration.

But don't let that scare you away from using tutorials. I credit a number of tutorials with helping me teach myself development. And I highly recommend them as a great place to start, especially when you want to learn how to code from scratch.

Reading

Next on the list is reading. Libraries could be filled to the brim with the number of programming books that are on the market. I have even written a few!

I like going through coding books because they allow me to go at my own pace. When I go through video tutorials, it usually means that I need to dedicate a specific amount of time to go through the videos each day. However, with a book I can read a few paragraphs or I can go through a few chapters. When you have a full-time job and you're learning programming on the side books are a great resource.

This is because they allow you to learn at your own pace. Books can also be a good resource later when you need to reference a specific topic. Also, when you go through a programming book I highly recommend you write and run the code from the book. This will help you remember the programming language syntax much better than simply reading it.

Remember that reading retention is incredibly low in most individuals. However, if you combine reading with actually writing the code as you're going through the content, you'll see much better results.

Another trick to use when reading programming books is to not look at the book when you're writing the code. For example, if you are reading my Ruby programming book you'll see a code snippet when you're learning how to use object-oriented programming. If you force yourself to type the code without looking at the book the entire time, you'll discover that your retention will increase dramatically.

Real-world projects

Last on the list to learn how to code from scratch is building real-world projects. After you've gone through a number of tutorials and read a few books, you'll be ready to try your hand at building applications.

A natural question to ask is: *"What types of projects should I build?"* There's really no right or wrong answer to this question. If you have an idea for a business then you could start with trying to build it with your newfound coding knowledge.

You could also look at re-building current applications, such as creating a Pinterest clone. I've found this technique of creating cloned sites very beneficial since it allowed me to focus on building functionality instead of having to waste time on coming up with ideas.

For example, when I learned the Swift programming language, I built an Instagram clone. Years ago, when I was learning HTML and CSS, I recreated the Google homepage from scratch. The most important factor to remember about building real-world projects is to stretch yourself. No developer ever improved by duplicating functionality they are already comfortable building. Instead, make sure you are challenging yourself to implement features that you've never created before.

Coding is hard

On a final note, don't let anyone tell you different: coding is hard! From setting up a development environment to building functional applications, programming will greet you with challenges at every stage.

But you can learn programming

However, with that being said, you can become a developer. There's not a magical programmer gene that coders are born with. It simply comes down to:

- How determined you are
- If you're willing to work consistently
- How good your strategy is when it comes to learning

48

How to Choose a Developer Specialty?

Through many years of training developers, I've discovered that it's vital for coders to decide about their specialty and focus. In this chapter, I'll share with you how I personally view the different developer directions and areas of expertise that are available.

You'll quite possibly make this choice more than once in your career as a developer, so I recommend that you always observe and be aware of the choices that can be made in your career.

How to choose a developer specialty?

The world of software development is so vast that it's impossible for someone to master every aspect of the process. Consider if I approached a world-class track and field coach and said that I wanted to train for the Olympics and win a gold medal in track and field. The coach would most likely give me a once over and chuckle to himself. But after that his first question would be: *"What event do you want to train in?"* He would ask this question because the training regime for the 100-yard dash is dramatically different from the high jump.

In the same way, as a developer, you need at least once, and quite possibly several times, to narrow your focus on what type of developer you want to be in the years ahead.

I'm going to walk you through each type of developer category so you can see what they entail.

#1 – the full stack developer

In deciding how to choose a developer specialty I always like to start off with the full stack option. I start with this option because many new coding students I've spoken with assume that all developers are full stack developers. And this is simply not true.

Full stack development means that you feel comfortable working with every stage of an application's development. Referencing our track and field analogy, a full stack developer would be like a decathlete. This is the category that I personally fall into. My focus on the full stack side of programming is due to a number of factors:

- To teach students and write development curriculum I need to be familiar with all of the key development types.
- I've spent years as a freelance developer. And in many cases, freelance coders are asked to build an application from the ground up, create all the features, design the system, and deploy it to the web or app store.

Full stack developers need to be a jack of all trades! Much like a decathlete, full stack developers are usually good at a number of technologies. However, a common pattern you'll see is that it's very difficult to be world class at *every* layer of the development stack.

Programming is simply too complex, and languages/frameworks change versions so rapidly that it makes it nearly impossible to excel at every stage of the app development life cycle. Because of how time consuming each level of the development process is, full stack developers simply don't have the time to become true masters at any one aspect.

As a full stack developer myself, I mitigate this issue by focusing my time on the components that I excel in, such as server-side development, and then working with other developers to help cover my weaker areas, such as UI/UX.

#2 – the server-side developer

Next on the list of developer types is server-side programming. This is probably my favorite layer of the developer stack. Server-side specialists spend most of their time working on building and implementing algorithms that enable programs to work properly.

Additionally, server-side developers typically spend quite a bit of time building APIs. This is because most server-based applications need to communicate with the outside world in some form or another. This layer of the development stack will require you to specialize in a language, such as Ruby, Python, Java, or C++.

#3 – the frontend developer

When it comes to choosing a developer specialty, the third layer to choose from is the frontend component. Not too long ago a frontend developer was considered someone who spent all day working with HTML and CSS. Their main goal was to make applications look *pretty*.

However, the definition of a frontend developer has changed dramatically with the advent of client-side frameworks. These frameworks, such as Angular and React, have made it possible for frontend programmers to build complete apps with little server-side interaction.

These applications are rendered completely in the browser because they're written in JavaScript. And whenever the app needs to get additional data it simply communicates with APIs. A common pattern that I work with is building a number of server-side Ruby applications and then having a single Angular frontend app that renders the user interface in the browser.

So, if you love building applications that users will directly interact with and the idea of working with APIs doesn't scare you off, frontend development might be the right choice for you.

#4 – the mobile developer

Next on the list of developer types is mobile. If the idea of building the next Angry Birds or Instagram excites you, the mobile development field may be a good fit.

Mobile programming used to be a very difficult field to enter. Only a few years ago you would have had to master multiple languages (Objective C and Java) to build smartphone apps. However, JavaScript frameworks such as Ionic and React Native have made it possible to use JavaScript to build apps that behave like native smartphone applications.

You can still use languages such as Swift, Objective C, and Java to build truly native applications. And there will always be a great set of jobs for developers who specialize in these languages. However, if you are a freelance or full stack developer, by leveraging a JavaScript framework you can build smartphone and tablet-based apps for all platforms.

And it's been my experience that the learning curve for these JavaScript frameworks is quite a bit lower than the traditional mobile languages. Additionally, you may have noticed that the tools used for JavaScript-based mobile apps and frontend programming are similar. Because of this synergy, I have had a number of developer friends who have moved away from server-side development and moved into frontend coding because it allows them to tackle building applications for desktops, tablets, and phones.

#5 – the data scientist

This used to be considered the data field, and a few years ago I'd have called this something like the data developer category. However, data and big data have rapidly morphed into the fields of statistic data analysis and using artificial intelligence, such as neural networks, to gain insight into the huge amount of information now available.

These new fields are changing the face of how we process data and understand information, and it's a huge new career field for developers to explore. Right now, the mathematics involved can be quite intimidating, so you'll need to decide if you're ready for some heavy math and deep algorithmic learning. The math is going to become more abstracted over time, and if you're drawn to the idea of artificial intelligence and deep algorithmic learning systems, this is certain an area to consider for an ambitious developer today. Some of the most modern Python libraries provide an excellent way for a developer to immerse themselves into this field.

Making the decision

If you are new to development, don't feel pressured to pick out a specialty immediately. Instead, my recommendation is to explore each type of development layer until you find a focus that you truly love.

In this chapter, I've provided a very high-level view of the developer types. However, in reality, you will need to become even more specific with your development focus.

For example, if you're a server-side developer, you may want to focus on building eCommerce applications or implementing accounting systems. If you are an aspiring frontend developer, you may want to become a world-class security specialist.

A key insight that I've discovered helps quite a few people, especially newer programmers, is to look at developer job boards. Job boards are great for listing out the specialties that companies are hiring for. And by going through a list of potential job descriptions it may help you figure out what you want to focus on next in your career.

49

How to Choose Your Next Programming Language?

We have discussed the importance of picking a development specialty, such as frontend, server side, or mobile. However, simply choosing a specialty is not enough. You also need to decide on what programming language you want to focus on for the initial, or next, stage of your career.

No book or guide can tell you what language you should learn next, of course. That's a decision that can be made only by your. So, in this chapter my goal is to help you decide how to pick a programming language based on your current objectives.

How to pick a programming language?

If you went through the exercise for picking your developer specialty, you will notice a similar pattern for deciding on a programming language. A quick perusal of Wikipedia will reveal that there are literally hundreds of programming languages to choose from. If you take the approach of looking at each language one at a time, you might be able to make an informed decision sometime in the next hundred or so years!

Since iteratively going through the full list of languages isn't practical, I recommend two processes for helping you decide how to pick a programming language.

The next job you want

First on the list is basing your programming language choice on the job you want. If you've heard the phrase *"dress for the job you want"*, it also applies to development.

For example, if you want to work for Microsoft or with Microsoft-based products it wouldn't make sense for you to spends years learning Python and Django. Instead, you will want to focus on learning the .NET development stack and languages such as C#.

This strategy can be smart in certain cases, such as with Microsoft, since there are countless .NET framework positions available on the job market. This means that even if you can't get hired on with Microsoft, you can still get a job for an organization that utilizes the .NET stack.

However, this approach doesn't work quite as well for more specialized languages and companies. For example, imagine that you spend years learning Facebook's flavor of PHP, codenamed HipHop. If you fail to get a job working for Facebook you will discover that not very many companies utilize the HipHop framework and your job opportunities will be limited. I view this approach as a bit risky because it tends to place all your eggs in one basket.

Your specialty

My personal favorite approach is to pick a language that fits in with your development specialty. I'm partial to this strategy because it's what I used in my development journey and it worked quite well for me.

Deciding how to pick a programming language based on your development specialty means that you look at the types of applications you want to build. And then you work backwards to put together a list of languages that are best suited for your objectives.

For example, let's take the case study of you deciding that your development specialty is going to be building big data applications. By taking this approach, you can dramatically narrow down the list of programming languages that fit with your goals. Many languages can perform big data processing, but only a few languages truly specialize in it, such as:

- R
- Scala
- Python

So, by looking at your specialty first, you have just narrowed down the list of languages from thousands... down to three.

Chapter 49

Specialty-based mapping

Since I find this approach to be the most effective, let's walk through a mapping of development specialties to popular languages:

- **Full stack development**: If you want to be a full stack developer, the Ruby on Rails stack may be the best choice for you. This stack offers a great set of tools for web developers and allows for the build out of robust applications.

- **Frontend development**: For frontend developers the path to follow resides on the JavaScript track. The JavaScript programming language has emerged as the clear winner in the frontend development space. And by becoming fluent in JavaScript you will be able to work with popular frontend frameworks such as React and Angular.

- **Server-side development**: The world of server-side development can be a bit intimidating. If you review the server-side languages you'll discover lower-level languages such as C, C++, and Java. However, programming languages such as Ruby, Python, and Go also specialize in server-side development.

- **The data scientist**: The world of data science can appear at first sight to have impossible demands on a developer to also be a high mathematician. However, if you explore the modern Python libraries, you'll find a rich set of ready-made algorithms so you can be creating your own neural networks and machine learning systems very quickly indeed. I'd recommend Python for this reason if you're already familiar with the language. If you have a bit more of a statistical background, then I'd recommend that you explore further how the R language can get a gateway into a new career path.

Through my programming journey, I have worked to specialize in one interpreted language and one compiled language. I chose Ruby for my interpreted language, and for my compiled language I started with C. However, I haven't found very many practical uses for my C knowledge over the years. Also, I have moved onto the Scala language since it is a good fit for building big data algorithms.

Summary

In summary, as with picking your development specialty, my recommendation to aspiring students is to experiment with a number of languages before deciding on which ones to learn extensively. There are a number of tools online that make it helpful to see a side by side comparison for various languages.

For example, one of the deciding factors that led me to learning Scala was looking through the Scala algorithm implementations on Rosetta code (https://rosettacode.org/wiki/Category:Scala). So, don't rush into picking out a programming language. Give the decision plenty of thought and research and you will put yourself in a better position for making the right choice.

50
Developer Soft Skills – Learning How to Gain an Edge in the Marketplace

I've talked quite a bit in this book about improving as a developer. Most of the time I focus on how you can learn new technical skills, such as becoming more proficient in a programming language or framework.

However, if you limit your knowledge to technical talent you will be decreasing your chances for success in the marketplace. In this chapter, I'm going to walk through five key developer soft skills that you can utilize to become a well-rounded coder.

Developer soft skills

The list of developer soft skills I'm about to present you is by no means comprehensive. But what it does offer you is a representation of the soft skills that I've personally used and had success with.

From being the IT Director of a national energy company in my late 20s to the CTO of a coding bootcamp with locations around the world, I've seen these skills help me at every level of my career. And as you'll notice, they have very little to do with actual technical ability.

As a caveat, I do not mean for this list to overshadow skills such as practicing clean coding habits or focusing on improving as a developer. Instead these skills should complement your engineering talent.

Writing

First on the list is the ability to write. In the book *Rework*, by *Jason Fried and David Hansson*, who are also the founders of Basecamp and the Ruby on Rails framework, wrote that one of the skills they look for in job candidates is their ability to write. This includes positions that you would think writing skill would be pointless, such as developers and system administrators.

Obviously, a developer needs to be able to be skilled as a coder. However, the book explains that if a developer can write, it is a sign that he or she is a good communicator. Writing skill doesn't mean that each memo you write has to sound like a riveting novel. Instead it means that:

- You can organize your thoughts properly
- You can communicate what you want to say so that others can understand

Conversation

Next on the list of developer soft skills is the ability to converse well with others. Now if you're like me, this is by far the most challenging skill on this list. If I had my way I'd stay behind my desk building applications all day and never interact with another human. It's simply the way I was wired, and I know I'm not alone in that desire.

However, conversational skills are an absolute requirement when it comes to advancing in your career. Whether you are a freelance developer looking for new clients or a software engineer looking to get promoted, you'll discover that the top prerequisite to your success is not technical skill, it's likability.

If someone likes you they are going to want to give you a chance to succeed. And one of the most straightforward ways to get people to like you is by becoming a good conversationalist.

Conversation tips

Thankfully, I've discovered that the system for having great conversations is pretty straightforward. Here are some tips that I've used to improve at this skill:

- *Think back through your life and come up with some entertaining stories about yourself.* People love stories, especially if they are funny. And I've discovered that telling a few well-timed stories has been able to get me in the good graces with CEOs and executives over the years.

- *Make the focus of conversation be on the other person.* People love talking about themselves, so by simply asking insightful questions you will be considered a great conversationalist... even though you let the other person do all the talking! Like your stories, come up with a list of questions that you can recall at a moment's notice.
- *Do not complain.* I have yet to find the person that likes to converse with someone who constantly complains. With that being said, countless people seem to enjoy bringing up every negative thing that has happened in their lives when they meet someone. The good thing about this is that if you can have a conversation without complaining you will stand out as being an upbeat and likable person.

Management

Moving down the list of developer soft skills, the next item is management. Now if you're an entry-level developer, don't tune out. Management doesn't have to mean managing people or projects.

When I say management, I'm referring to how you attack each task you're given. For example, if you are handed a new feature to build, do you jump right in and start coding? Or are you more organized with your approach? If a client or managers see that you take a systematic approach to every task you're given they are going to feel more confident giving you more responsibility.

To improve this skill, I recommend you read up on project management books or take an online course on the topic. The few days that you'll spend learning about management practices will help serve you well the rest of your career.

Design

Next on the list is design. In Scott Adams's (the creator of Dilbert) book *How to Fail at Almost Everything and Still Win Big*, Adams describes how knowing the basic fundamentals of design should be required knowledge for all engineers.

I can't tell you how many times I've heard a developer say something like *"design really isn't my thing"*. It's fine if your top skill isn't design. However, learning the basics of what qualifies as a well-crafted design takes such little work that anyone who doesn't learn about it is simply being lazy.

As a developer, if you haven't researched what it takes to create a good design, you are going to be quickly bypassed by others who read a single book on the topic. There have been multiple times early on in my career where I neglected design and it cost me dearly.

I remember one time where I spent weeks building an incredibly complex feature to only have management spend the entire meeting talk about how much they hated the design, while completely ignoring the actual functionality. If I would have spent a few hours to design the look and feel of the product the meeting and project would have had a more favorable result.

Public speaking

Last on the list of developer soft skills is public speaking. This may seem like a useless skill for a software developer. However, let me give you two scenarios to think about:

- In scenario 1 there is a brilliant developer with poor public speaking skills. When asked to present a project that he built, an incredibly well-built project I may add, the developer talks in a monotone voice during the whole presentation and the product demo is filled with him simply moving from one page to another.
- In scenario 2 there is another great developer. But this engineer has worked on his public speaking skills and gives a well-organized demo. His time in front of the room is filled with clear language, amusing anecdotes, and analogies for each feature to make the project understandable for everyone in the room.

If you were in the room, which one of the projects would seem more appealing? It doesn't take a MBA to know that the developer in scenario #2 will win each time.

Note that both the projects were great pieces of software. Like I mentioned earlier, soft skills are not a replacement for technical skills. They are something to layer on top of programming expertise. You could give a Steve Jobs-level speech, but if the product doesn't work it won't matter.

Becoming a better public speaker

Public speaking is ranked as one of the most feared tasks to perform. However, I can tell you from experience that you can improve at public speaking quite easily. There are two things that I've done to become a better speaker:

- I am a member at a local Toastmasters group. Each week I attend a group meeting where I can practice getting up and talking in front of a group of people. By simply forcing myself to practice this skill consistently my public speaking ability has improved dramatically.
- Additionally, I listen to one TED talk each day. The TED conference lectures are given by some of the most skilled orators in the world. By listening to a new talk each day, it has helped give me ideas of ways that I can craft my own speeches and it has helped to build a mental model for what makes a great speech.

The importance of soft skills

So, now that you know the list. How important are developer soft skills? I can't tell you how many times I've seen an inferior developer promoted to management simply based on their ability to speak well in meetings or converse with co-workers.

Remember that the key to each of the skills on this list is that they help people feel more comfortable being around you and that they will be confident that you can get the job done. Likability and confidence are two key prerequisites you'll need to gain an edge in the marketplace.

51
Developer Learning Options – A Practical Analysis

The entire world seems to be talking about the importance of becoming a coder. However, many of these discussions aren't practical. This chapter will walk through the various developer learning options available today, and help you decide on which option is right for you and your goals.

Degrees of programming expertise

If you're new to development the first task you should complete is to decide why you want to learn programming. There are a number of reasons for learning how to code, including:

- Becoming a professional developer
- Improving your skill in your current profession
- Learning for fun or for hobby projects

It's important to decide on your goals since they will dictate what learning strategy to take when it comes to how to learn programming. Let's look at each of them.

Becoming a professional developer

If your goal is to become a professional developer, congratulations! You'll be joining one of the fastest growing industries that the world has ever seen. The pay is great and the right developer jobs are both fun and rewarding. However, with all those benefits comes a strict set of learning requirements.

Pro coding jobs will require you to become proficient in a programming language and several frameworks. And simply building applications that function properly isn't enough for most jobs. Instead, you'll need to be able to build apps that follow processes such as:

- Test- and behavior-driven development
- Clean coding styles that are scalable and adhere to industry best practices
- Coordinate with developer teams and seamlessly work with code version control systems

And the list goes on and on...

Developer bootcamps

Any platforms or guides that say you can become a professional developer in a month or claims like that are simply lying to you. Becoming a professional developer takes years. I've been a developer for over a decade and I'm still learning each day. With that being said, if you want to make a career as a developer there are countless resources for achieving your goal.

Personally, I'd recommend starting with a developer bootcamp. Bootcamps allow you to become fully immersed in a language or framework over a course of several months. And many of them, including the one I run, DevCamp, offer job guarantees after you've completed the course.

These immersive programs aren't easy or cheap. They'll usually require around 40 hours a week of study and practice. And you'll find they range from around $5k to $20k. This may seem like a pricey option; however, how many training platforms can guarantee that you'll get a job after a few months of study?

Is this practical?

It may seem like I said a contradictory statement when I said that developer bootcamps can help you get a coding job in a few months. But I also said it takes years to become a professional developer. Let me let you in on a dirty little secret in the software world... many individuals working in developer jobs aren't professional programmers!

After getting hired from a coding bootcamp you'll most likely be a junior developer. The companies that hire bootcamp graduates understand that they're usually new to programming and they take it upon themselves to continue the new hire's education.

This is a win-win scenario. Developers can get great paying jobs with limited experience. And software companies can train developers to follow the procedures specific to their organization.

Improving your skill in your current profession

Another great reason for taking interest in how to learn programming is to improve in your current career. I'll give you a great example of how this can work. I have a good friend who spent his whole education focused on business. After graduating from college, he got a job working for an energy company and he realized he wasn't climbing the corporate ladder quite as fast as he wanted. He approached me initially to see what it would take for him to transition and become a full-time developer. After a few minutes of speaking with him it became apparent that he didn't really want to become a programmer, he was simply frustrated with his current job.

So, I began asking him questions about what types of tasks he had at work. He worked in the supply chain division for his company and it was his job to comb through fleet management data and generate reports. I proposed that he learn the basics of programming and then to focus on data science.

After a few months, he had successfully built a big data analysis program that was able to manage his entire division. When he presented his work to the company's executives they were so impressed with the program that he was promoted and given a hefty raise. When I talk to him now he doesn't mention leaving his job anymore. Instead he discusses how he loves it and how he's constantly looking for new ways to integrate automated mechanisms to improve the work he does.

Is this practical?

If you think this scenario fits with your goals. You can follow a much different path than professional developers. You can take online courses that walk you through practical projects that you can re-purpose for your own needs.

For example, the executive I just mentioned didn't learn how to build a machine learning algorithm from scratch. In fact, he'd be completely lost in even an entry level computer science class. Instead he took one of my programming courses and saw how the decision tree I built could be used in his division. After altering the data points, he could use it for his specific needs.

Learning for fun or as a hobby

This is a fun and relaxed way to learn. If you have a pet project that you've been wanting to build or if you simply like learning for the sake of learning, you'll discover a wide variety of resources that will help you achieve your goals.

When people ask me where to start when it comes to building code projects for fun, I typically point them to practical tutorials. If you're simply learning for fun you don't have to waste your time on complex computer science topics. Instead, you can focus on following step-by-step guides that walk you through how to build projects.

For these types of guides, you can access affordable ones on sites such as Udemy. The great thing about these types of courses is that they come with:

- Videos
- Written guides
- The source code for the project that you'll be building

This approach to learning makes for a great way to be introduced to development. And you never know, starting with hobby projects could end up with you going to the next level and learning professional programming.

Summary

In summary, I hope that this has been a helpful discussion on the various developer learning options that are available. I'd recommend checking out each option and taking an honest look at which one is right for you. No matter what you decide, learning how to code is a great experience and I recommend everyone to study it in one form or another.

52

Is it Possible to Lose Your Coding Skills?

This topic was inspired by a Boing Boing article (http://boingboing. net/2016/06/08/coder-fired-after-6-years-for.html) that tells the story of a QA developer who spent 6 years working for a company and literally did nothing besides playing computer games, browsing Reddit, and wasting his time.

The Reddit user, FiletOfFish1066, posted his story to the site and it instantly became a supreme case study for what happens when you don't continue to develop your coding skills.

After not working for 6 years, he says that he has completely forgotten how to develop and now he's out of a job. The story goes that he started working as a software tester and realized that, by writing some scripts, he could fully automate his job. So, he worked for about 8 months building testing scripts and after that he simply let the tests run. He didn't have to do anything besides kick back and play video games all day. There are a number of lessons that developers can learn from this story and that's what I want to cover.

I don't really blame the employee in this case. Apparently, there was such little oversight in his organization that he could get away with not working for 6 years. That tells me that the company he worked for has serious structural problems to let that go on for so long. It should be noted that many organizations are employing people to do work that software can do, but instead are choosing to waste money with archaic manual processes.

This developer started his job doing exactly what he should have done. He recognized that there was a way to automate his job, which was a great first step. If he would have gone to the management and shown what his automated script did, he would have most likely been promoted for his expertise and would have a great career right now.

It's possible to lose your coding skills. If a world class bodybuilder would stop going to the gym, eventually he'd lose his muscles. In the same way if you stop honing your craft as a developer, you'll eventually lose your programming skills.

A few years ago, I met with a gentleman who was the vice president of software development at a large energy services company. He got into the position by selling software that he had built himself, which has become the industry standard and currently processes billions of dollars in transactions each month. Even though this individual used to be at the top of his field as a developer, since he became an executive, he got further and further away from coding the application, and he admitted to me that he wouldn't even be able to build a simple program now.

I just finished reading the book *Peak* by *Anders Ericsson* and *Robert Pool*, and it gives case studies from the medical field, that show that the most experienced general practice doctors are not always the best in their field compared with less experienced physicians. The book explains that, on average, the longer a general practice doctor has been working in industry, the less they focus on learning and therefore they start to lose some of their expertise.

Surprisingly, it's actually doctors who have recently finished fellowships and gone through extensive training that perform the best. The authors did note exceptions when it came to specialists. For example, cancer specialists that perform surgeries daily and are constantly working on their craft, perform better than less experienced surgeons.

I thought that was a great example for developers because I know, from my own experience, that if I'm not daily using my development skills, they will atrophy. There really is no middle ground, when it comes to development you're either getting better or worse, you won't stay the same.

So how can you ensure that you're always improving and that you won't lose your coding skills? Here are a few practical tips that I use.

Chapter 52

Learn something new about development each day and be intentional with how you learn. In fact, just yesterday I taught myself how to integrate growl notifications into a Rails application (`https://rails.devcamp.com/professional-rails-development-course/advanced-user-features/how-to-integrate-growl-type-notifications-rails-app#.V2G-uD4TDUQ.twitter`), which was something I hadn't done before.

If you simply repeat the work you've done in the past, you won't improve. Thinking back to our case study of the general practice doctors, the research showed that the reason why the older physicians skills decreased was because they performed the same work day after day and eventually the only tasks they could perform properly were the things that they had repeated each day.

To be 100% honest, this part isn't very fun, which is why only a few people do it. Learning new and challenging skills can be intimidating and stressful. In the same book *Peak*, the authors said that a common trait among all top performers, in every field they researched, was that they were willing to deliberately practice skills that they found difficult, because it was only by mastering those skills that they could grow in their profession.

A practical way for developers to implement this method of deliberate practice is to write down a list of features that you have never built into an application before. Then, spend time each day until you have successfully built each component. After you're done with that list of features, create another list. I personally have a list that I work and study from and it's helped me to feel confident that I'm learning something new each day and that I'm constantly improving as a coder.

On a final side note, I've had multiple people message me about the story from Boing Boing asking how it was possible that the developer created a script for automating his work. Without further details, it's impossible to know for sure; however, since he was in the testing department my guess is that he built a test suite, using tools such as Capybara (`https://rails.devcamp.com/professional-rails-development-course/application-build/bdd-index-view`) to run through the software and generate reports on features. So that would be my guess.

Summary

I hope that this guide has helped to inspire you to be deliberate with your practice and that you will continually improve as a developer.

53

Is Writing Bad Code Immoral for Developers?

In this chapter I'm going to discuss a slightly odd question: is writing bad code immoral? This leads to the concept of the importance of developing well-written code.

This may seem like a weird question to ask because the mindset of most developers is that code projects are neither moral or immoral, they're simply programming files that perform various functionalities. I would like to think that most developers take pride in their work and therefore want to write code that adheres to best practices. However, given schedule and budget constraints many projects devolve, with the top goal becoming *to simply work* and being completed as soon as humanly possible.

However, this mindset can lead to issues such as: missing edge cases for features and poorly organized codebases that are difficult to maintain. Regarding the question of *is writing bad code immoral?*, I heard a great story from one of my Computer Science professors at Texas Tech, Dr. Michael Gelfond, which is where I got the idea to write this chapter.

During one of our lectures, Dr. Gelfond posed the question and then told a story. A few decades ago when he was a programmer working for a software organization, he ran into a nasty code bug. It took him several days to figure out that the previous developer had built a poorly constructed function that was causing the module that he was working on to break.

After Dr. Gelfond told us the story, he asked us again if writing bad code was immoral; most of the class answered that it wasn't. But then he asked if we murder someone a few days before they were going to die, "is that immoral?" To this, everyone answered with a unanimous "yes." He finished his lecture by saying, "Well wasn't it immoral that the last developer's code stole two days away from my life?"

That story and question has stuck with me for years, and now my answer to the question "is writing bad code immoral?" is a resounding "yes"! As developers, we should take pride in the work that we produce, not just for our clients' or employers' interests, but simply due to the fact that our goal should be to be true craftsmen in everything that we do.

Coding is the closest thing we have to magic in this world, and I feel honored to be able to work with it on a daily basis along with being able to teach others how to do the same. And with that in mind it should motivate us to have a clearly defined goal of being excellent at our craft.

One of my all-time favorite baseball players was Joe DiMaggio and he had a great quote that I think is very applicable to developers. He said:

> *There is always some kid who may be seeing me for the first time.*
> *I owe him my best.*

I try to apply this in all of the code projects that I do, it's easy to fall into lazy habits. However, I remind myself that someone might be looking at this project and it could be the first impression they have about me as a developer, and if I took shortcuts, even if the application works, it could reflect badly on the work that I do.

This doesn't mean that you can't make mistakes, quite the opposite actually. I'm constantly striving to become a better developer and because of that, I'm always trying to work on building features and projects that I haven't created before, which naturally leads to mistakes during the learning process. However, there is a clear distinction between mistakes that get made while you're trying to build an ambitious feature compared with project bugs that pop up due to laziness and poorly written code.

Chapter 53

How to write better code

So, if writing bad code is immoral, what can be done to combat it? Thankfully, we have a nice set of tools and workflows that can be implemented. Here are a few of the ones that I've found to be the most effective:

- **TDD/BDD**: Regardless of your thoughts on test- or behavior-driven development, there's no denying that if they're implemented properly it can lead to a well-constructed codebase. TDD naturally leads to following best practices such as low coupling and small methods, and with its refactoring step, I'm a huge fan of using it to ensure that an application is built the right way.

- **Continuous integration**: Assuming that you have a comprehensive automated test suite, continuous integration tools such as Codeship or Travis will make sure that code will not be pushed to production until it's passed the full test suite. I've had a number of times where Codeship has blocked a bad deploy that would've taken down a site. Additionally, it gives the development team a report on what needs to be fixed if a bad deploy is attempted.

- **Pair programming**: This is one of the most powerful tools you can use as a developer. If you're not familiar with it, pair programming is the process where you and another developer both take turns working on a project at the same time, preferably in the same room and on the same computer. When one of you is coding, the other developer is watching and giving advice or warnings. Whenever I'm building a complex feature, I will always use pair programming since it's akin to working with two brains on the same feature.

- **Continuing education**: No matter how long you've been a developer, you'll never reach a stage where the learning ends. Each day I try to learn something new, whether it's from tutorials, books, or blog posts from other programmers.

Summary

I hope that this has been a thought-provoking chapter and will help you on your journey towards becoming a code craftsman.

54

Inspirational Programming Advice from Howard Roark

In this chapter, I'm going to discuss one of the quotes that I've always turned to for inspiration as a developer.

It's from Ayn Rand's book, *The Fountainhead*. The main character in the book, Howard Roark, is a skilled architect and typifies the concept of being a true craftsman, in the same way that all of us, as developers, should approach our own projects.

This quote discusses how every project is special and deserves a unique implementation, and it goes as follows:

> *"Rules? Here are my rules: what can be done with one substance must never be done with another. No two materials are alike. No two sites on earth are alike. No two buildings have the same purpose. The purpose, the site, the material determine the shape. Nothing can be reasonable or beautiful unless it's made by one central idea, and the idea sets every detail. A building is alive, like a man. Its integrity is to follow its own truth, its one single theme, and to serve its own single purpose."*

> —Howard Roark, The Fountainhead

Even though this was written in the early 1900s and was for the architecture industry, Roark's approach to craftsmanship can be applied just as easily to programming. It can be easy to fall into the trap of staying in a comfort zone and simply duplicating implementation and functionality from project to project. However, that can create two problems:

1. You don't grow as a developer. The only way to get better is to step out of your comfort zone and build features that you've never done before so you can learn new concepts.

2. Projects suffer, becoming square pegs in round holes. Each application has its own set of unique requirements and therefore, should have a custom implementation.

I hope that you found Roark's wisdom inspirational and that you can apply it to your own development projects.

55
Best Practices Versus Creativity as a Developer

In this chapter, I'm going to discuss how you can find the balance of best practices versus creativity as a developer.

To be honest, this was initially a difficult chapter to write, mainly because I had a hard time organizing my thoughts on the topic since it's a little abstract. I had the high-level concept of the strained relationship between best practices vs creativity as a developer, in the sense that many developers, especially the ones new to coding who will fall into two camps:

- Those attempting to follow standardized conventions in every way, essentially duplicating code from tutorials and a language or framework's documentation page.
- Those ignoring all common practices and building applications in whatever way that makes the most sense to them (at the time).

There are pros and cons with both approaches, and like many other topics, a cross between the two is going to result in the best strategy. Let's look at the pros and cons of following best practices and ignoring the idea of being creative.

Pros:

- Application code will be easier for future developers to pick up and add features to since they'll know how the code is structured and where all of the methods and classes are located.
- Programs should be well-tested via unit and integration tests.

Cons:

- Code structure may have more of a cookie-cutter approach.
- Code may suffer from the square peg/round hole syndrome.

Before I go on, please don't misunderstand me by thinking that I'm saying that developers who follow best practices have these issues. I'm simply referring to developers who throw creativity out the door and simply try to build programs using standardized methods and attempt to copy code that they see from other developers.

Now let's take a look at the pros and cons of developers who only embrace creativity:

Pros:

- They have fun, this is very important since it keeps them motivated to build interesting projects. They're also able to express their unique perspectives on how applications should be structured.
- They're constantly trying new things and finding new ways to build features. This can result in learning quite a bit about the language or framework that they're using.

Cons:

- Programs that only rely on the developer's creativity can be nearly impossible to manage later. Even the developer who built the application may have a hard time understanding his own code if he has to go back and add new features.
- Even though programs built ignoring best practices and relying solely on the developer's creativity are fun to build at first, as the codebase grows the level of fun decreases exponentially. In fact, it's common for new developers to kill an entire project and have to start from scratch because the codebase became such a mess following a non-standardized approach.

So, if there are pros and cons to both approaches, which is the best way to go? I am a self-taught developer, and originally, I definitely fell into the second camp of building apps simply using creativity.

However, I ended up building some horrible applications, I did learn a lot about various languages through the process, so it was a beneficial strategy from a learning perspective. Over the years, since I matured as a developer, I realized that I had to find a balance between following standardized best practices and being able to add my own creative touches into a program.

Chapter 55

It's simply ignorant to disregard industry-wide accepted best practices. Concepts such as properly structured, object-oriented code increase a project's maintainability and also makes it more efficient to add new features in the future. Some of the most brilliant minds in the world have spent the past century refining development procedures, and a good developer should build upon that cumulative knowledge.

With all that being said, there is still a place for being able to integrate your own creativity into a development project. The more skilled I've become as a developer, I've realized that I'm more creative with my code than I ever was before. When I originally started programming, my *creativity* was really just an unorganized attempt to get features to work the way I thought they should be structured in my own mind. However, around a decade of experience has refined how I build programs, and that experience has allowed me to learn how to be more expressive with how I write applications.

The more confident I've become as a developer, the more I've been able to explore different ways of building projects and I'm having more fun now than ever I had before. I'll leave you with this thought from Sandi Metz, one of the software developers I personally admire the most and the author of the book *Practical Object-Oriented Design in Ruby* when she described the balance between following cookie-cutter approaches vs implementing creativity in development, she said:

> *"Design is not an assembly line where similarly trained workers construct identical widgets, it's a studio where like-minded artists sculpt custom applications. Design is thus an art, the art of arranging code."*

I hope that this has been a helpful discussion and will help you find the balance of best practices versus creativity as a developer in your own projects.

56
A Practical Guide to Approaching Project Development

One of my favorite parts of being a teacher is interacting with students. And this chapter will focus on answering a viewer's question regarding strategies to **approaching project development**.

Student question

The following is a letter I received from Christian, a developer from Germany:

Starting web development a year ago, I'm currently building my first own commercial product (a classified ad site) using Rails. I really would like to hear your advice on how you approach building features on apps, as I have the following problems:

I can't really plan a feature from start to end because I always think I'm missing something important

Procrastination and being afraid to make errors that will be costly to correct in the future

How do you approach building features when you don't know the scope exactly?

What`s your process, how do you get unstuck?

Best regards,

Christian

Strategies to approaching project development

In this letter, each of the questions revolve around having a strategy for approaching project development. And in this chapter, I'm going to walk through an answer for each question.

Planning a feature from start to end

The first question from our developer Christian asks:

> *"How do you approach building features when you don't know the scope exactly?"*

This is a great question. As helpful as it would be to have a clearly defined scope from the beginning of the project, it rarely ever happens. And even if you were given a perfectly crafted project scope, it would most likely change during some stage of development. This would essentially render the scope pointless anyways. In our developer's (Christian) email, he said he was building out a classified ads site, so we'll use that as an example case study throughout this chapter.

Moving from requirements to stories

One of the statements made was that you don't feel comfortable planning features from start to end because you think you're missing something. This is a common issue when you approach an application built based on a set of requirements. You probably tried putting together a list of requirements, such as:

- A user should be able to register
- Records can only be edited by the user that created the posting

If you take this approach, it's natural to feel like you're missing a feature, especially if you're new to development. Instead of using requirements, I'd recommend creating user stories. I'll give you one from a classified's app I built last year:

A user logs in to the application. From there, she sees buttons for creating new posts or editing ones that she has created before. She only sees posts that she personally created and she can't access this page without logging in to the app. In addition to seeing her posts, she can click on a post to review all the responses from users to that post.

Notice how much more practical this is than simply listing off requirements? Your app should have dozens of user stories that contain all the initial functionality that you want to build.

Starting with a base case

Now that your app has a nice set of user stories, how detailed should they be? Honestly, I would recommend that you keep the functionality as basic as possible. When I'm building applications, I don't even include all of the parameters that I know I'll need later.

When it comes to approaching project development I take a base case strategy. This means that I drill down a feature to its most basic component. Getting back to your classified ad app, let's say, it has a story such as:

When a user is on the page to create a new listing, she can add a title, a description, and up to 5 pictures. From there she can click on save to create the post, which redirects her to the post show page.

If you try to build that entire feature it would be very intimidating. So, my approach would be to first simply create a form page. From there I would only add in the ability to create a post with a title. The description can be added easily in the future.

Therefore, I don't see any point in wasting time on it in the beginning. I would completely ignore the picture uploading functionality in the beginning since that will require using tools such as nested attributes. So, after a user can create a post with a title I can circle back and add each of the other components one at a time. Taking this approach makes the entire process less intimidating.

Fear of the unknown

In the email, he mentioned being afraid of missing something important. This fear of the unknown is completely natural and let me say: you will be missing something important. Creating user stories should help to catch the critical items. However, I promise there will always be components that initially fall through the cracks. However, don't let that scare you off, you can add new features in later.

From my personal experience, I remember one time where I was building an enterprise application and completely forgot to give managers the ability to view posts they were supposed to approve! However, after I realized that I left out a key feature I could add it in and the client was happy.

So, don't let the fear of missing a key feature stop you from building. Remember the initial Facebook developer strategy.

Moving fast and breaking things

After becoming a public company, Facebook has moved away from approaching project development in this way slightly. However, when it comes to building applications it's still a strategy that I embrace. And I've discovered that it leads to getting more done. Additionally, moving fast and breaking things will also help remedy your second problem.

Battling procrastination

I greatly appreciate Christian's candor (which was a huge reason why I decided to give him a 1,500-word response instead of pointing him to some other resources). In the email, he admits to struggling with procrastination. And I'm glad that he did because procrastination is something that every developer I've ever known, including myself, have to fight against.

One of the top tools I use to battle procrastination is thinking small. We, as developers, naturally tend to push challenging features away. Instead, we like to focus on working with components that we're already comfortable with. That's natural for everyone, however it's not good. And I have to remind myself of this fact daily.

In his book *Deep Work*, Cal Newport discusses how deep work (the type of work that takes someone from good to great) is not fun. In fact, when researching top performers, Newport found that 100% of the individuals did not enjoy working on challenging tasks. So, when it comes to approaching project development, please understand that the scariest features might be your greatest catalyst for improving as a programmer.

Small, practical steps

So, my personal recommendation is that you embrace the difficult features, but take an incremental approach. For example, imagine that you're intimidated to build in the ability to let users upload multiple images per listing in your classified app. This feature can intimidate even experienced developers. You'll need to use nested attributes and incorporate a number of JavaScript elements to allow for dynamic behavior.

This is the type of feature that could lead you to procrastinate since it's a bit on the scary side. However, I'd recommend that you tackle the feature right away. You can write down a strategy for how you're going to build the component, such as:

1. Integrate nested attributes for posts.

2. Build a JavaScript script that can dynamically create new file upload elements.

3. Hard code some image URLs in a sample record in the database.

4. Finally connect the system to the storage engine.

And then guess what, you're done! Notice how much less intimidating the feature seems when you break it down into smaller steps? This is the key to fighting procrastination.

Getting unstuck

When it comes to development there are a number of ways developers can get stuck.

Application bugs

If you find yourself getting stuck on a bug, I highly recommend isolating the feature that isn't working. Too many times developers attempt to fix a component while still trying to keep the rest of the system functioning properly.

When it comes to debugging, I throw best practices and form out the window. Everything is on the table when it comes to fixing a bug. For example, if data isn't showing up properly on a page, put a database query in the view template. Gasp! Don't worry, after you've discovered what the bug is, you can then immediately refactor the code to conform to best practices.

Other techniques I find very helpful when it comes to getting unstuck is using the Rails console to run scripts and working with debugging tools such as Pry. These tools allow you to isolate the issue and focus on the problem instead of letting the rest of the application get in the way.

Messages over models

Lastly, a key differentiator I've discovered between good and great developers is in the way they look at application development. A good developer can look at a program or feature and start by listing out all the models, their attributes and relationships.

However, great developers first focus on the messages that will be sent from class to class. This is a completely different way to think about development. Instead of looking at classes like static object blueprints, it forces you to think about the actual behavior of the classes.

This isn't an idea I came up with. The esteemed developer Sandi Metz described this concept the best when she said:

> *"You don't send messages because you have objects, you have objects because you send messages."*

57

How to Practice Programming Techniques and Improve as a Developer?

Whether you are new to programming or have been at it for years, practice is important. The more you practice your programming skills, the better you will be. You have various options to practice programming techniques. These options will help you brush up on your skills and continually improve as a developer.

Engaging in pair programming

Programming doesn't have to be a solitary activity. Instead of taking in on by yourself, engage in pair programming. Since pair programming has people working together from a single computer, it is a great way to learn different strategies for tackling problems and approaching the process. This type of practice will quickly make you a better programmer, as long as you choose a good partner.

Utilizing open source software

Open source software is a great way to practice your programming techniques. Start by reading code from various open source projects. This will help you understand how the programmers managed to create such a successful project.

Then, participate in various open source projects. As you work, people will give you immediate feedback. It might be hard to hear the criticism from time to time, but it will help you fine-tune your skills, which will make you a better programmer.

Visiting the DailyProgrammer subreddit on Reddit

Reddit is a community full of people who share ideas and help one another. You can get in on the action with the DailyProgrammer subreddit (`https://www.reddit.com/r/dailyprogrammer/`). This subreddit posts three programming challenges each week. The first challenge is relatively easy, and then they increase in difficulty. The community reviews the solutions and provides feedback. Use this subreddit to improve your skills while having some fun.

Taking online courses

Sometimes you don't need to go back to school to develop your programming skills. **Massive Open Online Courses** (**MOOCs**) are an excellent way to brush up on your skills. You can learn at your own pace and practice the techniques that you need to work on without getting rushed. Best of all, you can get feedback during the course, which will help you become a better programmer.

You can check out my *Professional Rails Course* (`https://www.udemy.com/professional-ruby-on-rails-coding-course/`) if you want to learn how to best utilize the Rails framework.

Chapter 57

Code katas

The term kata was first introduced by *Dave Thomas* in the book, *The Pragmatic Programmer*. He borrowed it from martial arts and applied it to the programming world. To code katas, you need to take a small requirement and create the code. Then do it over and over again, improving it until it is perfect. This is an easy way to practice coding while making your code better.

Summary

Don't make the mistake of thinking that you don't need to practice programming. You should practice as often as possible. You can leverage these recommendations to practice programming techniques to improve your skills so that you can take your career or your hobby to the next level.

58

What Does It Take to Become a Great Developer?

Whether you've been programming for years or if you're just now learning how to code, it's natural to ask yourself: what does it take to become a great developer?

I'm going to start off by saying that there is no right or wrong answer to this question. If you ask 100 experienced software engineers this question, you'll get 100 different responses. The reason why there's no clear-cut answer is because development is truly an art. Therefore, asking this question about programming is similar to asking what makes a great artist.

Tips for becoming a great developer

In preparation for this chapter, I asked various developers, I read blog posts, and I listened to a number of podcasts discussing the topic. As I expected, the components of becoming a great programming are extensive.

In this chapter, I want to give an overview of the processes and requirements that I've found the most effective. The following are six traits that encapsulate the key characteristics found among great developers. I've also included some practical strategies for working with each of these attributes on a regular basis.

Working through difficult features

Starting off with one of the most challenging traits, I've found that the only way I improve as a developer is to work through challenging concepts.

I find it disturbingly easy to fall into a routine where I only perform the same tasks again and again. I've been working as a developer for a number of years and I therefore have a nice arsenal of tools and features that I'm comfortable building.

However, I've discovered that if I simply keep building features that I'm already comfortable creating, I won't grow as a developer. It's only when I bear down and dedicate myself to work through a difficult task that I've never performed before that I become better myself.

Having the requirement of working through difficult practice isn't a concept related solely to development. The book *Peak* by *Anders Ericsson* and *Robert Pool* researched peak performers in music, athletics, and essentially every other skilled profession. The results of the research revealed that individuals only show improvement when working through challenging concepts. This means that if concert violists played the same music day after day and never challenged themselves, their skill would stagnate.

The same concept holds true for developers. If you want to become a great developer, you need to work through difficult topics constantly. If you don't know where to start with finding challenging features to build, visit some of your favorite websites. You could look at Twitter, Airbnb, or Pinterest. From there you can compile a list of advanced features that you've never built before. Examples would be components such as: infinite scrolling, asynchronous notifications, or multi page authentication.

Community contribution

With the growth of the programming industry, the open source community has expanded exponentially. The most popular languages and frameworks in the world, such as Python and Ruby, were created not by corporations, but by programmers interested in the common good.

Depending on your level of experience, community contributions will vary pretty widely. If you're a senior-level engineer, you could build an open source code library or build a feature for a programming language. However, even if you barely have any experience, you can still contribute. New developers can assist other individuals who are just starting to code.

As great as it is to give back to the developer community, there are also significant benefits to contributing. If you're building a code library that other developers will see, you'll most likely be very careful to ensure that the codebase is properly tested and functions properly. This type of development will make you an even better programmer and will help you in the long run.

Artistry

When it comes to development, it's easy to get caught up in the day-to-day minutia of a project and forget that, at its core, programming is an art. For code to be artistic, it must be elegant, and for it to be elegant, it must be simple. Some of the best projects that I've worked on ended up having the most straightforward codebases. However, writing simple code is not as easy as you may think. Sandi Metz said this about simple code:

> *"Novice programmers don't yet have the skills to write simple code."*

Einstein said this about simplicity:

> *"If you can't explain it to a six year old, you don't understand it yourself."*

This may seem like an odd concept. However, if you've ever attempted to build a complex project that maintained an easy-to-follow code design you know it to be true. The more you improve as a developer, the most straightforward your work should be.

Craftsmanship

Craftsmanship is closely related to artistry. However, there is an important distinction. When you're a craftsman you truly take pride in your work.

Over the years I've met all kinds of developers—from programmers who simply treated each project like a widget on an assembly line, to developers who made sure that every code file they worked on looked like a piece of art.

Personally, I've found a cross between the two concepts to be the most effective. Like many other concepts, craftsman is not isolated to programming. Growing up, my Dad, who was a Major League baseball player and is now a coach, always taught me to have what he called a Spirit of Excellence. This meant that no matter what I did or what I was working on, I had to take pride in it. He would tell me that if I was taking the time to perform a task, I might as well do it properly.

While I feel that I take pride in my work, craftsmanship is one of the concepts that I struggle with the most. I find this principle challenging because it can be difficult to find the balance between well-written code and perfect code. As the saying goes, *perfection is the enemy of great*. Therefore, it's important to ensure that you work hard to properly design your codebase.

However, don't pressurize yourself to achieve perfection. It's also important to have the mindset that no project is ever truly completed. This means that if you attempt to achieve perfection you'll constantly be frustrated. Mainly, due to the fact that you will never reach a stage where your codebase will ever be considered done.

Steve Jobs's craftsmanship

When it comes to craftsmanship, few have taken the same level of pride in their work as Steve Jobs. This is what he had to say about craftsmanship:

> *"When you're a carpenter making a beautiful chest of drawers, you're not going to use a piece of plywood on the back, even though it faces the wall and nobody will ever see it. You'll know it's there, so you're going to use a beautiful piece of wood on the back. For you to sleep well at night, the aesthetic, the quality, has to be carried all the way through."*

> *—Steve Jobs*

Adapting to change

If you've worked on any real-world code projects you can attest that there is only one true constant: change. Great developers set themselves apart from novices by how they adjust to changing requirements for an application. There are two ways that new coders struggle with change:

- *No flexibility with the code design.* This means that when a new requirement is added to the project, they will need to completely reconfigure the code to allow for the additional functionality.
- *Planning for the wrong future.* A developer may have developed a mental model of what the end project will look like, however that estimation rarely matches reality. Imagine that you're building an accounting application and you think the client is going to eventually ask for the system to be completely project based. You will make design decisions based on the workflow hierarchy that you have in your mind. However, if you're wrong, you will be forced to reconfigure the entire application.

Both these pitfalls are normal to come across on a coding journey. However, a great developer finds the balance between no design and premature design.

By building well-constructed codebases, the great programmer writes modules that have flexible interfaces that can adapt to change. They also understand that project requirements change and that the code they write has low coupling.

This means that changes to one feature in the application should have little to no impact on other parts of the program. For example, back with the accounting application, if a change is required to the payroll module, it shouldn't require you to rewrite the personnel management feature.

Tireless learning

Lastly, in answering the question: "What does it take to become a great programmer?" I'm going to discuss the importance of tireless learning.

One of the most important factors in reaching your development goals is having a thirst for knowledge. Thankfully, you have 100% control over this requirement. Regardless of how much experience you have as a programmer, you won't ever reach a stage where you should stop learning. There will always be improved processes, new frameworks, and new languages to learn.

I've asked some senior developers that I work with how they organize their learning methods. They gave the following recommendations:

- *Learn one new language or framework each year.* This should also mean that you're building a production application during that year. It's easy to follow tutorials and build hello world applications. However, when you create a real-world program you'll be forced to work through challenging constructs.
- *Read multiple books daily.* I personally have over a dozen books that I read daily related to development. In fact, many of the topics that I discuss in this book were informed directly by the things I was reading at the time.
- *Follow advanced tutorials.* Many of the developers that I work with admitted that they prefer to learn new coding techniques by reading blogs from other programmers. There are a number of guides available online that you can go through that will teach you how to build advanced features into your applications.

- *Subscribe to newsletters.* I subscribe to a number of newsletters that are sent to me each week. This includes newsletters on Ruby, Rails, and JavaScript. These types of newsletters are a great way to stay up to date with changes in a language. They curate some of the best blog posts and tutorials from around the web.

Summary

I hope that this has been a helpful chapter and will help you answer the question, "What does it take to become a great programmer?"

59

How to Stay Sharp as a Developer?

When I think of the concept of **staying sharp**, images of focused skill come to my mind. From a programming perspective, a sharp developer is one who feels confident working with challenging projects and can calmly adjust to changing requirements.

I've mentioned in previous chapters that developers never remain at the same skill level. As a programmer, you're either improving or losing your expertise, there's no middle ground. So how can you stay sharp as a developer?

Tips to stay sharp as a developer

Here are my five great tips to staying sharp as a developer. If you follow these, you'll always feel ready to focus on the next goal or challenge in your career.

#1 – coding exercises

First on my list are coding exercises. At the end of the day, nothing is going to help you improve as a programmer as diving straight into the code.

You may think that working on work or hobby projects are enough to keep your skills sharp. However, it's been my experience that many of the projects I manage for work don't test my skill as a developer. There are exceptions of course, but much of the coding I do on work projects revolve around application configuration as opposed to algorithm design.

Growing up, I could watch the baseball players that my Dad coached. These were Major League athletes who were at the peak of their profession. I still remember how they stayed sharp as hitters. Playing in games was not how they improved, games were where they showed off their skill. Instead they became better players by going through drills and exercises that focused on improving specific components of their game.

In the same way, we, as developers, need to dedicate time on improving specific elements of our coding techniques.

This image is a GitHub gist of some coding exercises (https://gist. github.com/jordanhudgens/8033986) that I go through regularly. Above each code snippet is a task, and my job is to place the implementation code below the objective. These programming exercises force me to continually refine my skill and find new and better solutions to complex problems.

Example coding exercises

Some example questions could include:

- *Remove strings from an array that start with "system."*: This requires me to work with the array data structure, integrate a Regular Expression matcher, and know how to remove selected elements.
- *Convert an array of strings into a hash that has the string as the key and value as the string's length.*: This exercise forces me to understand how the Hash data structure functions, how to use the enumerable Map method, and work with blocks.

And the list goes on and on. I'm continually adding new problems to solve and I try to spend some time each day. Around 30 minutes to an hour working through these exercises. If you are looking for a great list of programming problems check out Project Euler (`https://projecteuler.net/`). There you'll find hundreds of great challenges that you can work through.

#2 – teaching others to code

Next on the list is to teach others how to code. I was homeschooled growing up, and at around age 12 I had to start teaching myself algebra. I initially struggled with learning new concepts and I was getting frustrated. My Mom realized that when I studied by myself I had a hard time understanding what I was reading. But it was when I explained the lesson to her that my comprehension skyrocketed.

She was teaching all of my siblings, so she couldn't be by my side all day. So instead, she got one of my sisters' dolls and sat it next to me at the table. She instructed me to read the lesson plan and then explain it to the doll.

At first, I thought it was the dumbest idea I'd ever heard. Explaining algebra to a doll, aptly named *Big Dolly* due to her size, seemed akin to a homeless person talking to himself at a bus stop. So, I did what every 12-year old would do and I ignored the advice…. Until I went through my next lesson and realized that I had no idea what I just read. So, after staring at the doll for a few awkward seconds I started to explain the concept to her. Shockingly, by walking through the lesson with the doll I started to understand it! And no one was more surprised than myself. So, *Big Dolly* helped get me through algebra, trig, and calculus.

How does this apply to development?

So how does my weird story about teaching a doll algebra apply to staying sharp as a developer? Well, when I started to learn programming I didn't pick it up right away. In fact, I really struggled with how to build applications. But then I remembered back to my high school math era. But instead of bringing Big Dolly back from the attic I started creating programming tutorials.

It was through teaching others that I started to understand development better than I ever have. In fact, the origins of *DevCamp* and *CronDose* can be traced back to my desire to improve by own skills by teaching others. So, if you're looking to learn coding or to improve as a developer, I highly recommend that you teach others and your own expertise will grow.

#3 – reading

Next on the list of tips for staying sharp as a developer is reading. I have a membership to Safari Books Online, which is essentially a Netflix for developers. Through that membership I have access to thousands of coding books. On my daily to-do list, I have around 7-8 books that I go through.

Sometimes I read a few small sections and other times I'll read a few chapters, depending on how much time I have. Going through development books has helped me continually refine my skills as a programmer and I'm constantly on the hunt for new great books to go through.

#4 – newsletters

Fourth on the list are development newsletters. I try to keep my time very focused. Therefore, I limit the number of newsletters that I subscribe to so that I can dedicate time to reviewing each of them when they get published.

Some of my favorites are the newsletters from: *thoughtbot* and *Codeship*. These types of resources contain comprehensive guides that will help give you a unique perspective on development and how to implement new features.

#5 – tutorials

Last on the list of tips for staying sharp as a developer are tutorials. Whenever I'm learning a new language or framework tutorials are one of my favorite resources for studying.

Screencasts are the closest you can get to having an instructor in the room with you. Providing you with step by step guides that you can follow to build applications from scratch. Thankfully, with the growth of the online educational industry there are tutorials for essentially everything that you want to learn.

Summary

I hope that this has been a helpful set of tips that will help you stay sharp as a developer, and good luck with the coding!

60

Developer Resume Tips – How to Create an Effective Resume?

Over the years, I've heard programmers say that they only need a resume if they want a normal job. However, it's been my experience that a resume is required for traditional job interviews, freelance clients, and even raising money for a startup. With that in mind I've put together this collection of **developer resume tips**.

Developer resume tips

I've been on both sides of the hiring process. I have been in the place of sending out resumes to hundreds of companies, hoping for a response. And I've also been on the receiving end where I was sent countless resumes from applicants.

The list I've developed has been fine-tuned throughout the years. With the strategies coming from the resumes that resonated the most with me along with the elements that worked best when I sent them to potential employers. In this chapter, I've compiled three straightforward developer resume tips that will optimally position you with hiring managers.

Keep it simple

Starting off the list is **keep it simple**. I have passed over many resumes that included pages of extensive descriptions and explanations of a developer's experience. If a developer sends me a resume that's over 1 page it's rare that I will take the time to go through the information.

The resume firm, Novorésumé, created a resume for Elon Musk where they condensed Musk's career down to a single page. And if Musk can have a single page resume, so can you. So, with this in mind, what pertinent should you include in your resume? A well-crafted resume will typically include information such as:

- *Your name and contact information:* You'd be shocked how many individuals will write multiple pages listing their accomplishments but forget to leave their email, phone, and social media links.
- *Your education:* And when I say education, I don't only mean traditional education sources such as your high school and college. The education portion of a resume should include any bootcamps or online educational institutions that you completed.
- *Your work experience:* In your work experience section, brevity is a virtue. Hiring managers don't want to read through every little detail of every project you've been involved in. They simply want to ensure that you will be a fit for the position that they're looking to fill. That's it. It's not that complicated.
- *Your skills:* Another common mistake I see from applications is forgetting to list out their full set of skills. As with all the other resume elements, keep this list simple as well. For example, I summarize my list of skills down to a few lines that discuss the programming languages and frameworks that I work with.
- *Your achievements:* Lastly, you should list out any achievements or certifications that you've earned in your career.

Keep it relatable

Next on the list is to **keep it relatable**. If you are applying for a frontend developer position, customize your resume to revolve around your frontend skills and experience. When I was sending out my resume to companies, I customized the content of the resume for each organization. If a company said that it was looking for a server-side specialist, I created a resume that highlighted my server-side expertise.

If you think that creating custom resumes is sneaky you'd be wrong. Hiring mangers typically decide on whether or not to contact you within a few seconds of glancing at your resume. By creating a custom resume that outlines a set of skills and experiences that fit the company's needs you are helping to make the hiring manger's job easier. So, it's a win-win scenario.

Chapter 60

Keep it professional

Third on the list of developer resume tips is to **keep it professional**. Companies hiring managers really could care less that you like animals or that you enjoy running marathons. You can discuss your hobbies during the interview process. However, on a resume, hobbies take up precious page real estate that can be utilized by listing out additional skills or experiences.

Summary

In summary, writing a resume is truly an art. Resumes should be succinct, customized to the job position, and clearly describe why you are the best person to fill a position. If you have never written a resume before, I highly recommend that you work with a service or individual that can help you with the process. Services such as Novorésumé are great for this type of work and you can also hire an experienced resume writer from sites such as Upwork for under $100. Considering that a well written resume can make the difference between getting a job or not, I think it's a wise investment.

61
Developer Salary Negotiation Strategies

Talking about money is a sensitive subject for many individuals, and when it comes to negotiating how much you'll be paid it also comes with the added stress of knowing that if you ask for too much you may not get the job and if you ask for too little it could negatively affect your lifestyle. With that in mind I've put together a list of developer salary negotiation tips.

Knowing your skill set

This may seem like common sense, however it's vital that you know and can articulate your full set of skills since this is going to be one of the main factors that dictate your salary.

You can start with listing out the programming languages you know, the frameworks that you've used, and put together a portfolio that showcases your expertise. As an example, if you're a full stack developer who also has experience with data science, you will be more a more valuable asset to companies that require a unique skill set like yours.

Knowing the industry

Over the years I've been fortunate to work as a VP of Engineer and a software Director in the oil and gas industry. The oil and gas industry has historically had a difficult time attracting software developers compared with other sectors, and because of that developers are able to command a premium salary. I would make a much different salary if I applied to work for the automobile manufacturing industry compared with the oil and gas space.

Therefore it's important to understand what industries pay for developers and not to simply assume that the same skill set is paid the same amount across all sectors.

Knowing the organization

No matter what your skill set is and what industry you're working in, no factor will determine your salary as much as the organization itself. If you're applying to work for a bootstrapped startup you'll be paid significantly less compared with a startup that just finished raising $20 million of venture capital.

It's been my experience that small to medium sized companies, with around 500-1000 employees pay the most. If you are applying to work with a bootstrapped startup, they may be willing to negotiate with stock options which could eventually lead to a much larger payday than any salary would, so that is also important to keep in mind.

Researching salary rates

With all of that in mind, how can you research salary rates? You can always simply Google *software developer salary* and then name the industry that you are interested in. Typically, career sites with job adverts will give you a huge indicator. However, I typically like to use *Glassdoor*, which I've found to have the most accurate salary rates.

You can also have Glassdoor filter by the location that you want to work in. One key item to keep in mind is to test out multiple job types. For example, when I search for *web developer* jobs in Scottsdale, AZ, it showed an average salary of $65,000, however when I looked up 'software developer' jobs in Scottsdale it returned an average salary of $78,000. That's a pretty big salary bump for a single word difference, so make sure that you check out all of the potential job types that you're interested in.

Another interesting option is to watch some of the yearly developer surveys that some large sites conduct, such as the annual developer survey at Stack Overflow. These kinds of surveys will break the industry down into various sectors and request information about typical salary rates. While you can't take surveys like this as facts, they are an excellent indicator.

I hope that this guide has given you a system for negotiating your next salary.

62

Best Questions to Ask During a Job Interview

In this chapter, I'm going to discuss the **best questions to ask during a job interview**, and I will also discuss the other side of the spectrum and list out some key interview questions to avoid at all costs.

If you haven't been through many job interviews for a while, or haven't really ever prepared for one before, you may have the thought:

"I thought the interview was about them asking me questions."

However, one very important, and many times overlooked facet of a good interview is asking strategic questions of the interviewer. In fact, Forbes researchers have outlined three goals that your questions should achieve:

- Make sure the interviewer has no reservations about you
- Demonstrate your interest in the employer
- Find out if you feel the employer is the right fit for you

Interviewers like being asked questions. The questions you ask can reveal quite a bit about yourself, good and bad, therefore it's critical to ask the right questions. If you don't ask an interviewer questions, he or she may assume that you don't really care about the job itself and you're simply looking to make enough money to pay your rent.

Interviewers want to find candidates excited about working with their company. Remember that if you're hired, you are going to be a reflection of the interviewer and will help or hurt their reputation. Anytime that I've hired an employee that turned out to be bad for an organization, the management has approached me and asked why I hired them and how did I miss their shortcomings.

I kid you not, I hired an individual for a job around five years ago that turned out to be a horrible employee and our CEO still gives me a hard time about the hire half a decade later! So, make sure to take all of that into account when you're interviewing for a position.

The following is a list of the best questions to ask during a job interview along with rationales on why they're good questions to ask. I've picked these up through my years as a manager for several software companies and through researching the topic.

Best questions to ask during a job interview

"How is performance measured for this position?"

This is probably my favorite question to be asked. It shows that the individual is not only interested in the job, but also wants to have an understanding of what it takes to be successful. A key component of this question is also that the question focuses on how the company measures performance. This will give you a good idea of how data-driven the organization is and focuses on the key metrics that are important to the company.

"What are some specific challenges that I will be tasked with?"

Asking this question will show that you are not naive and that you understand that the job will have challenges and that you want to prepare for them in advance.

"Are there any responsibilities with the position that were not mentioned in the job posting?"

This type of question will tell the interviewer that you're savvy and experienced enough to know that 100% of the requirements don't always make it to the job website. For example, the job may be a software development job, however they may also want you to perform search engine optimization on the web application. This question not only positions you well with the interviewer but also will help you understand the full set of roles and responsibilities that the position will entail.

"What is the corporate culture like?"

I like this question because it will give you a feel for how employees interact with each other and management, it will also let the interviewer know that you aren't purely looking for a 9-5 job, you are interested in working with the team and fitting in.

Chapter 62

"On average, how long do employees stay with the organization?"

Similar to the corporate culture question, this will subtly let the interviewer know that you are not looking for a short stint at the organization, but that you are looking for a long-term relationship with the company.

The answer to this question will also help provide you with the understanding of how tolerant the company is with regard to keeping employees. If the average employee has been with the company for only a few years there may be some issues causing the rapid turnover. Whereas, if employees stay on for over a decade, it's a good sign that the organization is a great place to work.

"Do you have any hesitations about my qualifications or experience?"

This is a bold question and you may or may not want to ask it depending on your confidence level. However, it will let the interviewer know that you're not afraid to ask tough questions and that you're willing to hear constructive criticism. I've personally never been asked this question by an applicant but I would admire anyone that would be willing to ask it.

Poor questions to ask during a job interview

You will want to stay away from questions that appear that you want to get out of work such as asking about the amount of paid time off, tiers of vacation days, and so on. It's important to know these parts of the job, however it will reflect better on you if you instead ask questions such as:

"What types of benefits are associated with the position?"

This question will get the interviewer to give answers to the PTO and vacation time without you coming across like someone who's already trying to see when they won't have to work, but still get paid.

Typically, you will also want to not ask questions that start with *why*, because *why* questions will immediately make the interviewer defensive and will give the conversation a feeling of being confrontational. These types of questions can usually be changed to start with *how*, which will tell the interviewer that you are wanting to know more about the company instead of accusing the company of doing something wrong.

An example of this would be *"Why does the company pay by check instead of direct deposit?"* This makes it seem like you're saying that the organization isn't staying up with modern payroll procedures (which may or may not be the case), however nothing good can come from this type of question.

Hopefully this gives you an idea of what questions not to ask, but just in case a few more case studies would help, here are some more questions that you should avoid:

"Is telecommuting a possibility for the position?"

If it was they would've already mentioned it, if telecommuting is your top goal you should consider freelancing.

"How much does the position pay?"

You should already have a decent idea of how much the job pays if you're interviewing for it. You can worry about the wage after it's been offered to you, it's never a good thing when the interviewer thinks that you're top priority is how much money you're going to make because they'll assume that you will leave the company if another organization offers you a modest raise.

"What type of hours would I be expected to work?"

Interviewers and managers hate this question! Based on the job you should already know this. However, you can reframe this question by asking something like *"What does a typical day for this position look like?"*.

Lastly, never ask *"How did I do?"* or *"Do I have the job?"*. Asking how you did sounds like you just finished a spelling test in 3rd grade and doesn't reflect much confidence. And if you had the job they would have told you. Wait and follow up with the interviewer in a week and you'll be considered a mature and experienced candidate.

Summary

I hope that this has been a helpful guide and will help you put together a strategy of the best questions to ask during a job interview. Many aspects of an interview aren't known going into it, however you will always have the ability to control the questions you ask, so it is good to put together a list of questions to ask so you can maintain some level of control over the interview process.

63

Answering in an Impossible Interview

Questions

How would you like to be asked this question in an interview:

"How long would it take to sort 1 trillion numbers?"

Or

"How many planes are there in the sky at a given moment?"

If that doesn't sound like your idea of fun you're not alone and many organizations have stopped asking impossible or seemingly impossible questions; however, there are still interviewers who like to ask them, so I thought it would be helpful to discuss.

First and foremost, if you get asked one of these questions, the interviewer's top goal is not seeing if you know the answer or not, instead they are looking to observe your problem-solving skills. Typically, the best approach is to take a systematic strategy so you can show that you have an organized thought process.

Answering impossible interview questions – case studies

Let's take the first question as an example: *"How long would it take to sort 1 trillion numbers?"* That seems like a challenging task until you establish a base case, such as: *"How long would it take to sort 10 numbers?"*

If you know your algorithms, you would most likely choose to use a sorting algorithm, such as *Quicksort*, since it has an average sorting time of $O(n \lg n)$, which would be $O(100 \lg 100)$ after swapping out n for the total number of integers. So, it's actually trivial to sort 1 trillion integers, since it would be $O(1,000,000,000,000 \lg 1,000,000,000,000)$.

In this question, the interviewer is first wanting to ensure that you know popular algorithms and that you have a clear understanding on which algorithm would be the right fit for the task.

For *"How many planes are there in the sky at a given moment?"* this is a guesstimate question and the actual answer doesn't matter at all, instead the interviewer wants to see how you walk-through an analytical problem and also how detailed oriented you are.

For this I would start by asking the interviewer filtering questions, such as: all the planes in the world or only in the US? Does this only include commercial planes or private jets and military aircraft? And questions that show that you know how to properly think through each of the parameters you would need to know to properly answer the question.

From there break down the problem into subproblems; for instance, if the interviewer says that they only want the list of commercial planes in the air in the US, then you can start to create an estimate on how many flights leave an airport each hour, set an average duration of the flights, and so on. Then you can multiply that base case by the estimated number of airports in the US and you will have your guesstimate, and more importantly you will show the interviewer that you have thought through the problem.

I hope that this guide has helped give you a strategy on **answering impossible interview questions** and good luck with the job hunt!

64

Greatest Weakness Answers for Coding Interviews

What's your greatest weakness? To be 100% honest, I'm not a huge fan of this question since it's a lose-lose question: if the individual being interviewed is completely honest, they probably won't get the job, and if they give a flat out lie it will be evident very quickly.

However, throughout the years I have had several managers ask me this question, so it's important to have a well thought out answer ready. Since I've been on both sides of the interview chair, I have put together a list of the worst ways to answer this question and then some of the best answers.

Bad answers to your greatest weakness

So first of all, these are the kinds of answers you should avoid to the infamous question about what is your great weakness when you're in that coding interview:

- *Hard time saying no*: This will say that you are weak and will take on too many projects, typically resulting in poor performance.
- *Can have a hard time staying on a single task*: This means you should probably either learn how to focus or that you are supposed to be an entrepreneur, working for a company usually means long hours on long, repetitive tasks, and if someone is bouncing from project to project they're not going to be a good asset to the team.

- *Can be arrogant*: I had a professor in grad school, Dr. Richard Gelfond, who is one of the most brilliant computer scientists I've ever known, who said this about arrogance: *"Being arrogant occasionally doesn't matter, but it's never good"*. An arrogant employee won't be able to work well with others and will have a hard time taking correction or learning anything new... because they already know it all.

Good answers to your greatest weakness

Now let's see some great answers to the question about what is your great weakness when you're in that interview:

- *Can be slow to take action*: This is an interesting answer because it could be a bad answer if you leave it at this since it might tell the interviewer that you are timid, which would be a poor character trait. However, if you follow it up by saying that you are very detailed and that before you start a task you want to have a clear strategy for how to move forward, that is an employee I want to have on my team!
- *Can be overly critical on myself*: This will tell the interviewer that you care about your work and that doing it well is very important to you. Make sure to follow up with how you're working on yourself so that you still are working on being a craftsman at your work but to not get on yourself for irrelevant reasons.
- *Can be quiet*: This is one of my favorite things to hear, assuming that the individual follows it up by saying that they can be quiet because he or she thinks that it's important to listen to all of the details of a project or challenge before giving an answer. This tells me that the individual is going to be detail oriented and won't miss key items because they were too busy thinking what they were going to say next.

I hope that these strategies help you answer the question of: What's your greatest weakness? And good luck with the interview!

65

Enterprise Software Job Strategy and Guide

If you're a developer and have worked with startups or freelance clients, you'll find that the world of enterprise software jobs is quite different, in both good and challenging ways.

Some of the pros to working in the **enterprise software industry** is that large organizations typically are stable, have systems in place for development, and allow you to specialize on a specific piece of functionality instead of having to cover the full range of software features.

Some of the challenges that are unique to enterprise development are that there is typically quite a bit of red tape for developers. If you're used to being able to grab any code library and stick it in your application you'll find that enterprises are pretty picky about what outside libraries you bring in. For example, I was just talking with a enterprise software developer a few days ago who expressed how frustrating it was that it took two months for his company to give him permission to use the jQuery library, which is one of the most commonly used user interface libraries in the application space.

So what types of questions should be prepared for when applying for an enterprise software job?

- Questions about how well you work with **formal processes**. Depending on the company's level of formality you'll most likely need to explain how you have worked with different project management processes such as Scrum, Extreme Programming, and processes such as that.
- At large enterprises software bugs can cause millions of dollars in damages, so the **testing systems** are typically quite thorough. With that in mind, make sure that you are prepared to answer questions related to unit testing and behavior-driven development.

- Considering that we're living in a **Microsoft-based enterprise world**, having a solid knowledge of how well you understand ways to integrate with Windows servers, Active Directory, and tools such as SharePoint will be very important. I've personally been asked how I would integrate Active Directory **single sign on (SSO)** into a Ruby on Rails application, along with how to run Rails on a Windows server during various interviews. And if you know the Rails development system you'll know that these are not standard requirements at all.

- As with most development positions, you'll also need to have a solid understanding of the **technical skills** of the position. This usually includes being able to give accurate answers to questions related to object-oriented principles and a walkthrough of popular algorithms.

The technical portion of interviews will most likely be specific to the job. For example, if you're applying for a frontend enterprise software job they probably won't ask you about Quicksort, but they will ask you about how to properly manage JavaScript callbacks.

Summary

Hopefully, these four areas of questions will help you prepare and feel confident about applying for an enterprise software job, and good luck with the interview!

Index

A

accurate freelance bids
  estimating 181, 182
advanced features
  managing 105
application development
    process 106
approaching project development
  about 231
  application bugs 235
  base case 233
  fear, of missing key feature 233
  feature, planning 232
  key feature, strategies 234
  messages, over models 235
  practical steps 234, 235
  procrastination, battling 234
  requisites 232, 233
  strategies 232
  unstuck, obtaining 235

B

balance of best practices
  cons 228
  pros 227
  versus creativity as developer 227
Basecamp 142-144
BDD 223
blogging 94
bookkeeping options
  about 149
  FreshBooks 150
  NetSuite 153
  QuickBooks 152, 153

Build reporting engine 63

C

class
  creating 85
  instantiating 86
client communication
  issues 177
  maintaining, with system 178
client conflicts
  managing, with strategies 159-161
clients
  constant proposals, sending 157
  friends and family 155
  network events 155
  obtaining 155
  obtaining, as freelancer 157
  obtaining, outsourcing services 156
  outsourcing services 156
  proposal material 157
  result 158
code
  better code, writing 223
  poorly written code, fixing 110
  refactoring 110
code faster
  about 53, 55
  Beethoven 55
  default mind 54
  hacking 54
  slowing 54
code learning
  deciding on 188, 189
  reference 187, 188

code libraries
  Devise 103
  Pundit 103
coding 196, 222
coding exercises
  reference link 248
coding interviews
  weakness 263, 264
coding skills
  about 217
  losing, possibility 218
  practical tips 219
compounded learning
  about 37, 38
  case study 38
comprehensive study system 19, 20
consistent study
  versus cramming 33, 34
continuous integration 223
conversational skills
  about 208
  tips 208, 209
cramming
  versus, consistent study 33, 34
creativity as developer
  cons 228
  pros 228
  versus balance of best practices 227

D

DailyProgrammer subreddit
  URL 238
  visiting 238
deep work
  action, taking 22
  definition 22
  distractions, removing 22
  strategy, for developers 22
  studying 23
demonstrations
  importance 131
design 229

devcamp
  URL 219
developer
  about 12
  significance 191, 192
developer resume, tips
  about 251
  professional 253
  relatable 252
  simple 251, 252
developers, characteristics
  adapting, to change 244
  artistry 243
  challenging traits, handling 242
  community contribution 242
  craftsmanship 243
  tireless learning 245
developer soft skills
  about 207
  conversational skills 208
  conversational skills, tips 208, 209
  design skill 209
  importance 211
  management skill 209
  public speaking skill 210
  public speaking skill, tips 211
  writing skill 208
developer specialty
  data scientist 200
  decision making 200
  frontend developer 199
  full stack developer 198
  mobile developer 199
  selecting 197
  server-side developer 198

E

effective study practices
  case study 18
  reification example 18, 19
enterprise software industry 265
enterprise software job
  questions, while applying 265, 266

expert positioning 95

F

fear of success
  hacking 63
forced repetition 89
freelance business
  blogging 94
  expert positioning 95
  open source contribution 95
  organically growing 93
  referral requests 94
  social media marketing 96
freelance developer
  about 137
  scope creep 137, 138
  scope creep, approach 139
  scope creep, requisites 138
  scope creep, sign off 139
freelance portfolios, examples
  about 163
  accounting application 164
  API tool, developing 164
  frontend application,
        creating 164, 165
  scheduling application, creating 164
  social network utility, building 164
freelance requirement elicitation
  about 128
  conclusion 130
  feature, adding 128
  feature, building 128
  feature, issue 129
  solution 129, 130
freelancing services 183
FreshBooks
  about 150
  drawbacks 152
  features 152
  working 151
Frustration Zone 44

G

GitHub 147, 148

H

hacking 62
hacking procrastination 61
hard way 19

I

impossible interview
  answering 261, 262
  case studies 261, 262
  questions 261

J

job interview
  best questions 258, 259
  poor questions 259, 260
  strategic questions 257, 258

K

Kanban boards
  reviewing 107
katas
  coding 239
Kouros
  mental models 58

L

LeanKit 145, 146
learning curve
  about 45, 46, 50, 51
  liftoff 46, 47
  twilight zone 48, 49
  zone 49, 50
learn programming 196
legacy application
  about 109
  practical tips 110

legacy application, tips
  about 112
  codebase, drying up 113
  new features, adding via TDD 112
  specific features, breaking out into
     microservices 112
  test suite, creating 112
legacy scenario 115
LinkedIn 184
loop
  executing 85

M

Massive Open Online Courses
  (MOOCs) 238
memorization
  avoiding 83
  copy/paste 82
  guidance 77
  patterns, finding 81, 82
  real-world example, taking 80, 81
  repetition 78
  short-term memory,
     versus long-term memory 79
  visual mental mapping 78, 79
  visual mental mapping,
     implementing 79, 80
mental models
  about 58
  for developers 59
  for Kouros 58
Microsoft-based enterprise
  world 266
mind works 12
  reasoning 13
  smarter approach 13
mistakes
  creating 73, 74
  force learning 74
  kill pride 74
multiple sessions 23
multitasking 25

N

narrowed focus 88
negative effects
  additional 19
NetSuite 153

O

online courses
  utilizing 238
open source contribution
  about 95
  direct code contribution 95
  pre-existing libraries,
     contributing 96
  tutorials 96
open source software
  utilizing 238
outsourced web developers
  applications, accessing 180
  automated testing 180
  daily reports 180
  managing 180

P

pair programming
  about 223
  engaging in 237
perfectionism
  hacking 62
plan
  hacking 63
plateau
  false ceiling 42
  learning 41
Pomodoro Technique
  implementation 71
  lifestyle of productivity 71
  lifestyle, versus fads 70
  using 69, 70
PowerPoint 134, 135
practical system 55

procrastination
  coding steps 66, 67
  hacking 62
  instant gratification 66
  issues 65
  root causes 61, 62
prodigies
  about 7
  developers 8
  Mozart case study 7, 8
  tipping point 8
prodigy myth 8, 9
profession
  practical 215
  skill, improving 215
professional developer 213, 214
  developer bootcamps 214
  practical 214
programming
  inspirational advice 226
programming expertise
  degrees of 213
  learning 216
programming language
  learning 85, 86
  selecting 203
  selecting, based on development
     specialty 204
  selecting, based on job 204
Project Euler
  URL 249
ProWorkflow 146
public speaking
  about 210
  tips 211

Q

quality
  versus speed 120
QuickBooks 152, 153

R

Rails application
  reference link 219
Rails framework
  online reference 238
reading 195
  significance, for developers 37-39
reading schedule 39
reading system 39
real-world projects 196
Reddit
  about 238
  DailyProgrammer subreddit,
     visiting 238
Red, Green, Refactor workflow 169
refactoring
  80/20 principle, analyzing 116, 117
  architecture, changing 118
  automated bug list, building 117
  client, becoming 117
  fear factor, removing 116
  language/framework, moving 118
  versus starting over 116, 118
referral requests 94
referrals 184
reification example
  controller 18
  model 18
  view 19
remote desktop
  about 133, 134
  free options 134
  GoToMeeting 134
  screen sharing 134
reverse note taking
  about 88
  benefits 88
  forced repetition 89
  narrowed focus 88
  story-based mindset 89
running man 12

S

salary negotiation, tips
  industry, knowing 255
  organization, knowing 256
  salary rates, researching 256
  skill set, knowing 255
scope creep 137
screencast 132, 133
SEO, best practices
  about 173
  backlinks 175
  focused content 175
  relevant content 173, 174
  site responsiveness, managing 174
  site speed, managing 174
  text, images, and videos, mixing 174
  XML sitemap, creating 174
services
  review, to remotely demo work 132
silver bullets
  code libraries 103
  customization 102
  issues 101, 102
single sign on (SSO) 266
skill plateaus
  about 43, 44
  best practices 42
  challenging 43
  obtaining 42
  proper information/resources 42
small bites 193, 194
social media marketing 96
specialty-based mapping
  about 205
  data scientist 205
  frontend development 205
  full stack development 205
  server-side development 205
speed
  versus quality 120
starting over
  versus refactoring 116

staying sharp
  about 247
  code, teaching 249
  coding exercises 247, 248
  coding exercises, example 248, 249
  development newsletters 250
  reading 250
  tips 247
  tutorials 250
story-based mindset 89
system
  for decreasing task
     switching costs 26
  studying 15, 16

T

task switching costs 25
test-driven development
    (TDD)
  about 167, 121, 223
  choice, consideration 121
  client, decision 121, 122
  common sense, using 122
  decision, creating 121
  documentation 170
  development process, leading 170
  for coders 167-169
  importance 169, 170
  on freelance projects 121
  regression 170
  team management 170
tipping point
  doubt machine 4
  for developers 3
  own experience 4
  painful process 4
  tipping point(s) 4-6
top project management tools
  about 141
  Basecamp 142-144
  GitHub 147, 148
  LeanKit 145, 146
  ProWorkflow 146

Trello 144, 145
Wrike 146
traditional note taking
issues 87
traditional study habits
limitations 17, 18
Trello 144, 145
tutorials 194

U

updates
client update, automating 124
client update, example 124
importance 123
version control 124, 125
Upwork 106, 183
urgent client
about 97

employee, treating 98
firing 98, 99
toxic environment 99
tyranny 98

W

willpower limits
about 27, 29
copycat 30
decision, making 28
executing 29
focusing 30
importance 28
outfit 30
saving up 29
Wrike 146